D1595756

The Celebration of Society

The Celebration of Society:

Perspectives on
Contemporary Cultural Performance

Frank E. Manning

Bowling Green University Popular Press
Bowling Green, Ohio 43403

Congress of Social & Humanistic Studies
University of Western Ontario
London, Canada N6A 5C2

Culture and Performance

Frank E. Manning, Series Editor
Ray B. Browne, Associate Series Editor

Cover design by Paul Schuplin

Contents

Acknowledgements

All of the essays are original contributions to this volume. Oral versions were first delivered at various symposia and lectures sponsored by the Canadian Ethnology Society, The Association for the Anthropological Study of Play, or the University of Western Ontario. I thank my fellow contributors for their cooperation, comments, and patience.

I am indebted to many people for assistance in preparing the volume for publication. Sharon Wyatt typed the manuscript. John Cesarini and Doug Hagerman developed some of the pictures, and the Calgary Exhibition and Stampede provided the pictures in chapter 8. Sonia Kuryliw Paine copy-edited the text. Gail Manning organized the bibliography and helped to prepare the two indexes. Ian and Josephine McFadyen checked sources and read a final copy of the page proofs. To all, many thanks.

The Congress of Social and Humanistic Studies has been supported through the Academic Development Fund at the University of Western Ontario.

This book has been published with the help of a grant from the Social Science Federation of Canada using funds provided by the Social Sciences and Humanities Research Council of Canada.

Frank E. Manning
1983

Foreword

When anthropology emerged as a field of study more than a century ago, it was infused with a variety of humanistic disciplines: social and political philosophy, classical and religious studies, literary and art criticism, folklore, popular culture (though it was not called by that name), history, linguistics, law—the list goes on. Regrettably but perhaps inevitably the academic development of all these disciplines led to their splintering and specialization. Anthropology was gradually redefined as a science, and the humanities became compartmentalized and isolated from even their closest cognates.

Recently, however, the wheel has begun to turn again. Anthropology and the humanities are being reintegrated, and in the process there is a promising mutual revitalization. A growing number of scholars are rejecting disciplinary endogamy, along with its sterile pedantry and intellectual incestuousness, in favor of an eclectic liberal arts approach to the study of humankind. We are gaining a renewed appreciation of the creative, if not always measurable, aspects of human endeavor, such as religion, aesthetics, popular culture and play.

This series focuses anthropological and humanistic perspectives on cultural performance, a rubric encompassing ritual, ceremony, pageantry, popular and folk theatre, sporting and entertainment productions, ethnic, regional and arts festivals, and similar genres of collective symbolic expression. These dramatic spectacles are approached as dynamic arenas where sensitivities and meanings are generated, experienced, communicated, and acted upon in many ways. Analytical emphasis is given to how cultural performances reflect, interpret, and influence their society.

A book on celebration is an especially appropriate introduction for this series. Like the rapprochement between anthropology and the humanities, especially the new humanities, the contemporary florescence of celebration helps to restore a wholistic understanding of the human situation. Celebration reminds us that human life is less rational, secular, materialistic, and technologically determined than was commonly thought a generation ago; that we continue to cherish myth, rite, identity, community, tradition, cosmos and many other symbols and sentiments tinctured with the acquired wisdom of the species; that we remain *homo ludens*, not simply *homo sapiens* or *homo faber*; that we delight in fun and laughter, relish mischief and mystery, and are inspired by paradox and ambiguity; above all, that we seek recurrently to appreciate the wonder and beauty of the human experience, and to reward ourselves for bearing with it.

Frank E. Manning
University of Western Ontario

Prelude

The title of this book is intentionally ambiguous. It suggests both that society celebrates, or expresses itself, and that society is celebrated, or made manifest. The two processes are at play, ethnographically as well as semantically. In their dynamic reciprocity, we begin to see the significance of celebration.

The leitmotif of our essays is the relationship between celebration and the social realities of those who experience it. We view that relationship as both interpretive and instrumental. In its interpretive role, celebration is a distinctive part of the cultural repertory through which a people gain perspective on their situation. Celebration is fun, but it is also a performative statement, or "metastatement," about the social order. In its instrumental role, celebration is an important, often crucial, means through which people proclaim their identity and fashion their sense of purpose. Not infrequently, it is in the celebratory arena that a cultural community becomes an interest group, mobilized to pursue political and economic objectives.

The interpretive and instrumental roles of celebration tend to be particularly significant in contemporary societies and among those whose lives have been substantially affected by the complex and contradictory forces of modernization. Indeed, one of the striking characteristics of the contemporary scene is the burgeoning of new or revived celebrations. We set out here to examine this phenomenon cross-culturally and thus to contribute to a broader understanding of celebration, as well as of the social underpinnings of modernity. Both concerns have been conspicuously neglected by anthropologists, but warrant high priority on our research agendas.

Part I

Introduction

Chapter 1

Cosmos and Chaos: Celebration in the Modern World

Frank E. Manning

> A public celebration is a rope bridge of knotted symbols strung across an abyss. We make our crossings hoping the chasm will echo our festive sounds for a moment, as the bridge begins to sway from the rhythms of our dance.
> Ronald Grimes, *Beginnings in Ritual Studies* (1982:231)

I

At the Calgary Stampede, sterile bulls are paraded in public, while Canada's most powerful and wealthy politicians pretend they are cowboys, fighting the eastern Canadian establishment. At *Carnaval* in Rio de Janeiro, black slum-dwellers and mobsters have free reign over the city, while international celebrities clamor to be allowed into their ranks. On religious holidays in Sierra Leone, prepubescent boys dress up as devils and symbolically undermine the adult world; failing to get the message, their elders applaud the show. Every Saturday afternoon in North America, "good guys" and "bad guys" square off in wrestling matches that have been rigged, usually in the bad guy's favor; audiences are powerfully addicted to these exhibitions, and often enraged enough to assault the winner. At cricket festivals in Bermuda, high-rolling black gamblers chauvinistically display themselves as "bad-ass niggers," but get their betting money from whites. In small towns in Ontario and Minnesota, residents stage an annual festival in which they pretend they are living in the past and the surrounding society on which they depend for their livelihood is virtually nonexistent. In an urban center on the Canadian Prairies, Indian politicians stage a powwow that purports to represent ancient cultural traditions but which began as a media event for white consumption and is also aimed at bridging the social gap between reserve Indians and their middle-class leaders.

These and similar spectacles examined in the following pages exemplify what our epigraph suggests: the tenuous, subjunctive, paradoxical character of celebration. These qualities have so far not lent themselves to social analysis, which has been preoccupied with normality and predictability. Yet the humanistic revitalization of anthropology has shown us that human life is a precarious and wondrous balance between what Levi Strauss (1966) calls the "classificatory urge"—the penchant for logically structuring and regulating the cosmos—and what Peckham (1965) terms "man's rage for chaos"—a mischievous, sensual delight with irregularity and misrule. Encompassing order and disorder, celebration resonates powerfully with the polarities of the human condition.

What constitutes celebration? Four central features of the genre emerge clearly in this volume. First, celebration is performance; it is, or entails, the dramatic presentation of cultural symbols. Second, celebration is entertainment; it is done for enjoyment—for the fun of it—however much it is tinctured, consciously or unconsciously, with ideological significance or pragmatic intent. Third, celebration is public. The word itself means, *inter alia*, to proclaim openly and to achieve renown. Celebration socializes personal meanings, enacting them on the street, on the stage, in the stadium. There may be an admission fee, but there is no social exclusion. Fourth, celebration is participatory. Increasing professionalism notwithstanding, celebration actively involves its constituency; it is not simply a show put on for disengaged spectators.

The florescence of celebration in contemporary societies is truly striking and is the focus of our investigation here. Throughout both the industrialized and developing nations, new celebrations are being created and older ones revived on a scale that is surely unmatched in human history. As celebration is built on paradoxical ambiguity, its vitality in the modern[1] world constitutes a further paradox. The celebrant takes "time out" from practical affairs and ordinary routine, and does so openly, consciously and with the general aim of aesthetic, sensual and social gratification. Yet such conduct flaunts both the hallowed Western work ethic and the many kindred ideologies, political as well as religious, advanced elsewhere in support of development and modernization.

As colonialism contributed to its own subversion, modernity has undercut many of the values which fostered it. The phenomenal growth of leisure in contemporary societies has provided one of the more obvious contexts in which celebration is flourishing. The issue of leisure, however, is more complex than it may at first seem. It is not necessarily that we have more time free from work than those who lived in traditional societies; Norbeck (1974:35-39) has already shown that the reverse is often the case. Rather, as Dumazadier (1962) argues, leisure in the modern sense has a distinctive meaning: leisure is time that is separated from work, spatially as well as temporally, and over which the individual rather than society exercises control. Modern leisure is seen as the reward for work and is thus deemed an appropriate occasion for expending and enjoying income gained from work.

This understanding of leisure points to another contemporary phenomenon—the transition from producer to consumer capitalism. Abt and Smith (1983) indicate that it is not only commodities and services that are bought, but also, and more significantly, experience. We seek novelty, amusement, and a sense of "action," and view money as an appropriate means of purchasing it. Although they make this argument with reference to contemporary America, it obviously has wider applicability. One of the remarkable features of many Third World nations is the extent to which they have idealized a consumer lifestyle that imitates, and often exaggerates, American stereotypes.

The relationship of leisure, consumption, and cultural performance highlights MacCannell's (1976) provocative and intriguing theory of modernity. He underscores the central importance in the modern world of what he calls "cultural productions"; these are dramatic presentations encompassing (1) a model (an embodied ideal, or 'model for'); (2) an influence (themes, norms, and motivations deriving from the model);

(3) a medium (the communicative context of the model and influence—in our case, a celebration); (4) an audience (fans, constituencies, followers); and (5) a producer (those who create, control, direct, and enact the presentation).

MacCannell's use of the term "cultural production," which includes celebration, is deliberate. Challenging orthodox Marxism, he argues that in modern societies it is cultural productions, not economic productions, that have superceded traditional social relations as a basis of shared values and sensitivities. Cultural productions have become the generative basis of myths, lifestyles and even worldviews. Instead of social formations giving rise to symbolic expressions—the nexus identified by Durkheim (1915)—it is now symbols that are creating social groups. Social entities arise, and often develop an amazing, if ephemeral, solidarity because they share interests deriving from television programs, movies, sports, entertainment and so on.[2] "The modern world," reflects MacCannell, "has the capacity to organize itself around ideas, especially the ideas of bourgeois idealists" (1976:85).

This understanding has been echoed by others, and is now an item of conventional wisdom in anthropology textbooks (e.g., Kottak 1978) as well as in much popular-culture writing. For the moment, let it lead us to the two broad questions underlying our analysis: What does celebration mean? What does it do?

Our approach to meaning draws heavily on a line of thought traceable to Bateson (1958) and made more explicit by Geertz (1972). Celebration is a "text," a vivid aesthetic creation that reflexively depicts, interprets and informs its social context. In MacCannell's terms, celebratory symbols are the model(s). They subsume the social experience of the celebrants, cast it in dramatic form, and communicate cognitive and evaluative influences.

Our approach to the function of celebration draws both on Turner's extensive work on social drama (1957, 1974a) and on Cohen's (1974) "two-dimensional" elaboration of that perspective. We view celebration as a significant pause and point of reference in processes of a more mundane nature, and as a dynamic, often instigative force in a field of action. The way in which celebration articulates and modifies power relations is our special focus, which involves examining the political (in the broadest sense) relationship between "audience" and "producer."

The ambiguity of celebration affects both its textual portrayal of society and its active role in the social process. As a communicative agent, celebration embraces two modes: play and ritual. Play inverts the social order and leans toward license, whereas ritual confirms the social order and is regulated. The two modes are complementary as well as contrastive, and the tension between them gives celebration much of its piquancy and power.

Yet the balance between play and ritual also varies in ways that correspond with other factors. One of these factors is the modern system itself. Modernity seems clearly to favor ritual in celebration, whereas play thrives where modernity has been kept relatively at bay. Throughout this volume we find the most ritualistic celebrations in those cultures where modern values are central and strong. Conversely, ludic celebrations enjoy particular popularity among those whose relationship to modernity is more marginal and uncertain: Third and Fourth World peoples, and, within the metropolis, 'minority' races, classes, ethnic groups, and age strata.

Another striking correspondence centers on the distribution of power within the orbit of celebration. When those who control celebration are also those who dominate the social order, there is a tendency to ritualize that dominance in order to sustain and legitimize it. Conversely, when those who control celebration are in a socially subordinate position, there is a tendency to emphasize the playful devices of negation, such as reversal, irony, and the juxtaposition of social forms. Often, of course, the question of celebratory control is itself ambiguous and negotiable. Dynamic celebrations are symbolic (but important, and quite "real") battlefields for waging competitive struggles for power, prestige and material objectives.

The following, then, are the themes guiding our entrance into the celebratory genre: its paradoxical ambiguity, its significance as socio-cultural text, its role in sociopolitical processes and its complex relationship to modernity and hierarchy. These themes constitute a conceptual center from which our cross-cultural studies radiate.

We begin by examining two phenomena that are currently

popular in North American society: community festivals and
professional wrestling events. From there we move to the
cultural celebrations of three non-Western societies that have
recently and rapidly undergone modernizing changes: (1)
festival gambling in a Caribbean country that has been
nominally democratized; (2) *Carnaval* in a Latin American
nation that has been extensively industrialized; and (3)
children's masquerade pageants in an urbanizing West
African country. Then we return to North America, to the
internationally famous Calgary Stampede and to one of the
most renowned celebratory performances of native Indians,
the powwow. As we progress through the book we follow the
advice of the Indian scholar M. N. Srinivas, who urges anthropologists to become "thrice born": once in their own society of
actual nascence and growth, a second time by coming to terms
with another culture, and a third time by returning to their own
society and applying the anthropological perspective to it.
With this third birth, "We find that the familiar has become
exoticized; we see it with new eyes. The commonplace has
become marvelous" (Turner 1978a:xiii).

II

Community Festivals

Town celebrations are undoubtedly North America's most
widespread and familiar type of festival. Although sometimes
appearing "corny" in the eyes of an urban sophisticate, these
events generate intense interest among the local citizenry,
enlisting the active participation of vast numbers of them and
the active support of most of the rest. Old Home Week in Mount
Forest, Ontario is a good example, offering "something for
everybody, and everybody doing something."

To an astute anthropologist, the town celebration is as rich
in meaning as a Naven performance in New Guinea or a mock
rebellion against the Swazi king. Carole Farber examines the
four-day event as a collective *rite de passage*. The first day's
activities articulate the town's links to the national society,
chiefly through public education, but then proceed to separate
the town through the dramatic mechanism of a costume ball in

which the celebrants "become who they are not." The middle or "liminal" phase fills the second and third days, which are highlighted by two parades. The first parade is made up of floats sponsored by political leaders, prestigious voluntary associations, and, most importantly, established, family-run businesses. Held at mid-day on Main Street, its mood and content are sober. The second parade is a marked contrast. At midnight of the third day the citizenry assemble in their sleepwear and merrily move to an arena on the outskirts of the town where they enjoy an all-night dance. If the first parade epitomizes hierarchy, the second evokes egalitarianism. This sense of camaraderie prepares the celebrants for a reaffirmation of their ties with the larger society, the theme of patriotic events that conclude the festival on the fourth day.

Farber outlines a central tension from which the celebration derives its social significance. Until about 1970, the Mount Forest economy consisted of locally owned retail businesses and manufacturing firms that dealt with "natural," locally available materials: agricultural produce, wood, animal hides, gravel, water, and so on. More recently, Toronto and U.S. investors have bought into the retail sector, and branch manufacturing plants dealing with synthetic products have come on the scene. Fiercely proud of their traditional autonomy and self-reliance, Mount Foresters now face the unwelcomed reality that they no longer control the town's economy.

But that reality is excluded from what Farber calls the "official town ideology"—a social identity and value system based on what is deemed "good, stable, natural, and true." This ideology is symbolically constructed by extending the past into the present, showing that the town's heritage is an ongoing, timeless experience. The meaningful process at work (play) here is also characteristic of traditional celebrations. As Metraux puts it: "Traditional feasts and festivals constitute, symbolically, a way of recalling the origins—whether mythical or historical—of a community of men. They are occasions when cultural and national identity can be reasserted and feelings of self-awareness and participation in common experiences reaffirmed." (1976:7)

For Farber, the semantic highlights of the Mount Forest festival are the two parades, the first representing the town ideology's formal structure and the second its informal ethos. Notably, the outside businesses and their personnel are conspicuously absent from these parades, whereas former residents who have come "home" for the festival are prominently included. The celebrants are eventually returned to the wider society, this time with cultural resources that they may use either to resist external influences or, alternately, to negotiate and compete on behalf of local interests. Like traditional *rites de passage,* then, the festival strengthens its constituents in their inherited culture.

A thousand miles and an international border from Mount Forest, the farming town of Foley, Minnesota is strikingly similar. Robert Lavenda describes the community as having a strong legacy of parochialism that has been eroded as increasing numbers of Foleyites take jobs in new industries, commute to a nearby city to work, and marry exogamously. Foley's summer festival, Fun Days, recognizes the town's links to the surrounding region in the opening and closing phases, but the middle phase, which is protracted and more important, has a separatist theme. Lavenda sees the festival's overall character as "inner-directed."

The processual similarity between the Foley and Mount Forest events suggests that the *rite de passage* format may be a common pattern in community festivity. In both cases, moreover, the liminal or "seclusion" phase is highlighted by a profusion of kin-related symbols. In Mount Forest these are family businesses, "natural" products, and the festival itself, Old Home Week. In Foley's "inside" activities there is a clear differentiation of sex roles, almost a kind of Batesonian schismogenesis. Men are supervisors and in charge of events that require strength and technical skill, while women run the art and craft exhibitions and the children's program. Foleyites view this as a "natural" distinction, but, as in Mount Forest, kinship and nature have economic significance. The sexual division of labor in festivity is also characteristic of the traditional organization of farming.

Lavenda contrasts Foley Fun Days with Waterama, the summer festival of neighboring Glenwood. Waterama is choreographed not only for the townspeople, but also for visitors from other parts of Minnesota and surrounding states. Whereas the organizational style of Fun Days is personalistic, amateurish, and informal, Waterama is run in a bureaucratic, professional, and show business manner. Briefly, then, the Foley festival images a stable culture wedded to town-based conventions—a culture that is no longer entirely consistent with the community. Contrastingly, the Glenwood festival images a consciously changing culture that takes its cues from corporate, media-oriented mass society.

Lavenda emphasizes the role of each festival as a text about its community's internal social relations and its identity vis-a-vis the outside world. But each festival is also a dynamic force within a social transition that can be loosely described as modernizing. In Foley, Fun Days stubbornly reacts against that transition; in Glenwood, Waterama actively encourages it.

Sporting Spectacles

The opposition between the Foley and Glenwood festivals is symptomatic of a more general field of conflict and uncertainty. Throughout North America old values have lost much of their credibility and force, and newer ones have yet to become legitimate, as Jim Freedman's study of professional wrestling shows. Wrestling thrives in small towns, particularly in those where powerful outside influences have undercut local social structures but where conduct is still carefully scrutinized and righteousness expected. It also thrives in urban areas, notably among the underclasses and those who, like the constituency of country music, retain "small town sentiments." The world of wrestling fans no longer works as it should, but they are powerless to change it and limited by their own conservatism in understanding it.

Wrestling is a show as much as a sport. It is built on stock characters, scripted action, and an outcome that to many seems predetermined. Freedman explains that the central conflict in the ring is between a "good guy" and a "bad guy." The good guy's symbolism draws on themes that are highlighted in the liminal phase of conservative small-town festivals. Relying on his "natural" abilities, and claiming to fight for family and loved ones, he has the solid support of the audience. His opponent, the bad guy, relies on dirty tricks and artificial devices, and boasts of fighting for money alone. The audience loathe him. But fan popularity is not reflected in the outcome. The bad guy usually wins, partly because the referee fails to see and stop the violations of rule that are obvious to everyone else.

What, then, is the attraction of this maddening spectacle? Wrestling defines, dramatizes, and thereby renders meaningful, central frustrations of the audience (cf. Barthes 1972). It does not resolve the dilemma it poses but "rings true" to experience and is valued for that quality. To paraphrase Geertz (1964) on the role of ideology, wrestling "casts personal feelings into public form and endows private sentiments with social significance." It is a "map of social reality" and a "matrix for the creation of collective conscience."

Freedman suggests that the wrestling match is also an allegory of the modern capitalist state. The good guy is the working class, struggling to follow the rules and steeped in the belief that hard work and honesty will prevail. The bad guy is the capitalist class, pretending to observe the rules but relying on sophisticated ruses to conceal real motives and actions. The referee is the government, put there by the people to ensure law and justice but incompetent and suspiciously aligned with big money interests. The audience is itself, a disillusioned and enraged public. Liberal democracy, the social philosophy of capitalism, is on trial here, and it fails. The audience have no recourse but to take matters into their own hands, vigilante style—a course of action to which they are frequently incited at ringside and, afterwards, on the streets.

As a parable of power relations, wrestling is comparable to gambling in Bermuda. The popular game is crown and anchor, and it goes on at festival cricket matches in a large tent, the "stock market," where high-stakes betting is combined with the flamboyant display of sexual assets, the conspicuous consumption of liquor and *ganja,* and a great deal of spirited sociability. Blacks comprise the majority of the players, and today run most of the boards as well. A small number of boards are still run by Azorean Portuguese, Bermuda's entrepreneurial minority. Everyone knows, however, that whereas the Portuguese boards are independently financed, the black boards are bankrolled by leading white businessmen or racially mixed syndicates. The operators are merely their visible partners.

It is apparent that the Bermudian scenario is symbolic of much else. I am struck particularly by its affinities to the political system. Until the advent of universal suffrage a generation ago, Bermuda was controlled completely by a white merchant aristocracy known as the "Forty Thieves". Since then it has been governed by a single political party that claims to be a "partnership" of the races. The party is predominately white and white-financed, but it assiduously courts blacks with offers of high-profile positions and lucrative economic opportunities. The black party has no such largesse, of course, so it has keyed its appeal primarily on racial solidarity and moral integrity.

The stock market can thus be viewed as a ludic rendition—exaggerated but clearly recognizable—of the Bermudian political world. Blacks can play the public role of high rollers, but big money and effective power—as well as the social "odds"—remain in white hands. Blacks gain materially through partnership in the system, not opposition to it. It is a cynical message, of course, but its influence cannot be overlooked. Bermuda is the only democratic country in the world where a black majority has failed to win a popular election.

Like wrestling, then, gambling portrays the experience of its constituents as they deal with a power structure. Also like wrestling, gambling is viewed pejoratively by the respectable and righteous segments of society. In the case of wrestling this stigma seemingly involves a paradox, since the fans identify with the morally good antagonist. The gamblers, however, have a more ambivalent view of themselves. Evangelical Protestant values have shaped their lives, and unquestionably remain their most cherished moral ideal. They know deep down that the revivalist churches speak the truth, and that the stock market belongs to the devil. But they also recognize that temptation is strong, particularly during the festival season, when the lure of a quick dollar and the other delights of the stock market are attractive enticements to sin. The cost of compromise with the devil may be a loss at the crown and anchor board, but many blacks also see a more exacting price: their persistent inability to escape from political clientage. Interestingly, the black political party strongly supports the anti-gambling stand of the black churches, and pressures its members to refrain from involvement in the stock market, whereas black members of the government party are among the prominent board operators and big gamblers. Both groups "read" the stock market scenario as a political "text," but respond to it in different ways.

Masquerade Shows

Victor Turner's interest in symbolic expression has taken him through the forests of Ndembuland, along the pilgrimage trails of the world's major religions, and now to the Rio *Carnaval*. Replete with the creative fantasy of masquerading, an extraordinary measure of license, and an infectious spirit of *communitas, Carnaval* is the epitome of antistructure. Yet although the festival may appear simply to happen, like an annual miracle wrought by a *deus ludens*, it is one of the most elaborately organized events that one could imagine. The remarkable samba schools that produce the music and the masquerade troupes are hierarchically rigid, bureaucratically regimented, protocol-laden institutions. Turner's point is that it takes a good deal of structure to generate anti structure, and that play forms like *Carnaval* are often a complex combination of both. In Caillois' (1979) terms, *Carnaval* encompasses *paidia*—the capricious abandonment of play—and *ludus*—the rules, often extensive and intricate, which "contain" play and constitute the structural organization of the play world. Celebrations like *Carnaval* are thus a larger-than-life portrayal of both order and disorder, and in that sense a caricature of the human situation.

The vivid contrasts within *Carnaval* assume additional significance in the processual context of Brazilian life. In the seasonal cycle *Carnaval* gives way to Lent, a transition that juxtaposes a period of indulgence and extraordinary vitality with one of penance, abstention and pervasive reminders of death. But *Carnaval* does more than make the rigors of Lent bearable. It also renders them meaningful, in much the same way that the Fall gives meaning to the Redemption.

Carnaval may also have an important role in contemporary social processes. The samba schools are run by blacks and mulattoes, and located in Rio's worst slums. Yet the powerful mobsters who control gambling—a pastime that is "king" in Brazil—assiduously court these schools, hedging their bets on an uncertain future. Mulatto women, clad in bikinis (or less) are archetypes of aesthetic and libidinal attraction. Whites and visiting dignitaries pay handsomely to masquerade and socialize with them, offering strong social evidence about the appeal of non-white culture. Although *Carnaval's* role in this situation is conventionally seen in terms of symbolic, temporary rebellion, one should also consider the festival's potential to support, even mobilize, political movements aimed at democratic change—movements of the type that flourish in modernizing societies like Brazil.

The politics of celebration steps to the fore in Jeanne Cannizzo's analysis of West African children's masquerading. In Bo, a small but growing city in Sierra Leone, pre-adolescent boys enliven Muslim and Christian festivals by performing on the streets as *Alikali Devils*, the generic term for child-maskers. There are four masquerade motifs. The first two embody agility and beauty, qualities that the maskers idealize and unabashedly associate with themselves. A third devil represents power, normally a quality of the adult world but used in the masquerade to attack and undermine adults. A fourth devil, known as the *Kaka*, (literally "shit devil,)" is a clown figure—dirty, shabby and clumsy in appearance and performative style. The shit devil contrasts with, and lampoons, the other devils, but it also caricatures the child's view of adulthood, for, as Cannizzo explains, "Maturation is a process of decay. The *Kaka* is the senile, incontinent, palsied apogee of adulthood...." Notably, the performance concludes with the *Kaka* being captured and led away by the other maskers.

Children's play has far greater social significance than is generally appreciated. Cannizzo's analysis is built on the contrasting social positions of the members of the dance group and their parents. The parents are migrants to the city, but remain rural and tribal in their outlook, while the children are "urban and urbane." The generational difference is heightened by a further conflict. On the one hand, the children are influenced by the modern, Western notion that childhood is a separate social category, unlike the traditional conception of children as small-scale, submissive extensions of their parents and elder kinfolk. On the other hand, the children recognize that the realities of their urban situation, chiefly the need to go to school, make them economically dependent on their parents and subordinate to them to a greater extent, and for a longer period, than in traditional settings. Like black Bermudians in the stock market, these youths are torn between cultural solidarity and the constraints of their economic position.

Celebrating the culture of childhood, the masquerade performances serve the political interests of children in several ways. First, they articulate children's aspirations to be independent from their parents and from traditions which stifle the nascent cultural autonomy of the pre-adolescent peer group. Second, the masking troupes crosscut the inherited social boundaries of language, ethnicity, and religion, welding a cohort of children into what Cannizzo terms a "new tribe" or "interest group." Third, the performances depict children as powerful and stylish, and adults as impotent and silly, a social reversal that suggests vicarious retribution and that leaves open the possibility of the children's eventual triumph. Interestingly, masquerades are watched by adults, whom the children pretend to amuse in return for donations of money. The audience see the spectacles as colorful and humorous pageantry, but generally fail to recognize themselves as the objects of satirical attack in the *Kaka* performance. It is a double joke, as subtle and sophisticated as any produced by adult society.

Power Plays

Celebration is both culture and politics, or, better perhaps, cultural politics. The phrase implies two converse processes. The first is the politicization of culture, the translation of cultural symbols, beliefs, and values into political discourse and strategy. The second is the rendering of politics— ultimately, a matter of "whose ox is gored"—in cultural terms. As several of our papers propose, celebration is a kind of "power play," a dramatic arena in which cultural politics assumes style, shape, and significance. This perspective receives its most extensive treatment in studies of cowboy festivities and Indian powwows, two of North America's most distinctive and prominent celebratory occasions.

If the Bermudian stock market comically pretends to be

"Wall Street" but is ultimately a political theatre, the Calgary Stampede purports to be about livestock—rodeos are the major events—but is actually about the financial stock market, or, more precisely, about a society made rich and rather bumptious by its booming, oil-based economy. Herman Konrad summarizes the Stampede paradox with two oxymorons: barren bulls and charging cows. In livestock breeding a barren bull is useless, and would not be kept, much less paraded in public, as is done in the rodeos. But the bull also represents a thriving investment situation, or "bullish market," a meaning much closer to current social reality. Similarly, while cows are normally peaceful, they will charge to protect their vital interests, such as the welfare of offspring. Thus it is not really bulls and cows that are on display in the Stampede, any more than it is really cocks that fight in Balinese villages (Geertz 1972). The key actors are the human beings whose lives are caught up in these anomalous spectacles.

Proclaiming itself "the Greatest Outdoor Show on Earth," the Stampede is ostensibly a celebration of the frontier and ranching tradition. According to Konrad, however, the festival's only authentic link to the past lies in its perpetuation of Calgary's long-standing fondness for energetic self-advertisement and local boosterism. The Stampede was started by an American interloper in 1912, a decade after the demise of cattle ranching in southern Alberta. Even in the nineteenth century, Calgary was never a 'cowtown' to the extent of other early settlements in the American and Canadian West.

Yet the Stampede has become, to borrow Konrad's pun, a "sacred cow." For ten days each July the city is given over to rodeos, barbecues, square dances, and cowboy parades. Residents are encouraged to wear western garb, on and off the job. City employees and many workers in the private sector are given time off to attend events. The media establishment are unfailingly laudatory in their coverage, and editorialize that it is everyone's civic duty to display the Western image.

The historical fiction represented by the Stampede draws its significance from an underlying social discrepancy. Calgary has long sought, and largely enjoyed, the economic benefits of modernization. But it has also sought to distinguish itself culturally from eastern Canada, which it identifies with federal power and sophistication; in order to do this, it has adopted "wild west" imagery popularized by the American media. The Stampede symbolizes both objectives. It is a big and profitable business, thoroughly modern in its corporate public-relations techniques and its value as a tourist attraction. The Stampede also portrays the romanticized frontier, highlighting its ethic of toughness, its gregariousness and informality, and its axial figure, the colorful and daring cowboy.

Like the Mount Forest town celebration, then, the Calgary Stampede presents a kind of "official ideology" that obviates a social irony by creating a notion of the past and extending it into the present. The ability to understand and project this ideology—to manipulate it, one might say—is crucial in Albertan politics. Konrad cites the cases of Don Mackay, who introduced the white cowboy hat to Stampede imagery, and went on to serve a decade as mayor of Calgary, and Premier Peter Lougheed, who cut his political teeth on Stampede organizing committees, and remains a shareholder in the festival. At the same time, the Stampede ideology legitimizes Alberta's militant stance toward the federal government in the battle for control of petroleum resources. Spearheading this battle, politicians like Loughheed associate themselves with Stampede symbolism, both in their own constituencies, where it is a matter of survival, and in bargaining with Ottawa, where it gives cultural sanctity and force to *realpolitik*.

The political functions of the Stampede are replicated in another cowboy festivity, this time in the Yucatan village of Copal. Each May, the highlight of the Holy Cross fiesta is a mock bullfight. The 'bull' (which is barren, as in Calgary) is a colorful costume worn by a man who engages in stylized combat with a *vaquerro* (cowboy). Like the Stampede rodeo, the mock bullfight is an ethnohistorical drama. It emphasizes what the Mayans regard as their crucial cultural distinctiveness from the larger Mexican society.

Prominent patronage of the mock bullfights is an important political steppingstone in Copal, as in the case of the Calgary Stampede. The more poignant comparison, however, lies in the common role of these cowboy shows as the symbolic dimension of regional struggles for autonomy versus federal governments seeking greater political centralization and greater authority over the disposal of resources. The social processes which pit region against nation are imbued with cultural significance and influenced in political direction by what happens in celebration.

Politics is also an important dynamic of the Indian powwow. Unique yet broadly similar to a variety of performative traditions, powwow emerged in its present form in the 1950s and rapidly gained widespread popularity among North American Indians. Typically held on summer weekends, powwows are camping festivals highlighted by feasting, story-telling, games, musical performances, generous 'give-aways' of food and consumer items, and easy-going sociability. The strong appeal of powwow is indicated by its ability to attract Indian visitors from a diversity of linguistic, tribal, and social class backgrounds, resulting in a "powwow circuit" that reaches from the Canadian Prairies to the American Southwest. The powwow thus exemplifies what Durkheim (1915) regarded as one of the major attributes of religion—the bringing together of normally isolated groups to celebrate, and indeed create, their corporate existence.

Dealing with an urban powwow in Saskatchewan, Noel Dyck considers how the festival facilitates two major political goals of its organizers, who are the leaders of a local Indian association. Educated, urbanized, and the beneficiaries of "affirmative action" programs, these leaders are frequently viewed with suspicion by reserve and lower-class Indians, who see them as "brown bureaucrats." Powwow enables its organizers to counter this stigma by demonstrating their skill at running a popular Indian event. As Dyck puts it, "By hosting their own powwow, they (the Indian leaders) endeavored to show their guests that they are Indians who respect powwow and know how to perform it properly, in spite of the fact that they live in an urban center." Enlisting support through their involvement in celebration, Indian leaders stand on the same political ground as office-seekers in Calgary or Copal.

Besides gaining support from their Indian constituents, the Indian leadership seeks to project their personal prestige and the overall strength of their organization to the wider society. The powwow studied by Dyck had its origin as a radio and television program, and subsequently admitted whites to some of the dances and musical shows. To the white audience these performances convey a sense of the cultural resilience, social solidarity, and potential power of the Indian movement, enhancing the bargaining position of those who represent it. The politics of powwow, then, is situated in its organizers' role as brokers between native and white cultures. As this role is characteristic of Fourth World leaders (Paine 1971), it is likely that Dyck's observations and approach are generalizable and that celebration may be viewed as a stage on which definition and legitimation of brokerage relations operate in day-to-day life.

III

Play and Ritual

Recent work on festivals and popular spectacles has emphasized their use of inversion and license. Geertz (1972) argues that the cockfight provides a "metasocial commentary" by implicitly contrasting the absoluteness of an ascribed, immutable caste system with the radical shifts of social prestige accomplished in the momentary span that it takes a gamecock to tear its opponent to pieces and a gambler to lose or gain a substantial fortune. Turner (1977) emphasizes the "anti" or "meta-structural" character of festivity, its proclivity to transform and transcend the structural arrangements, behavioral requisites, and normative principles that prevail in ordinary situations. Babcock (1978) contends that the conventional world is "reversible" and that the spirit of festivity, exemplified in a wide variety of artistic and sociocultural productions, achieves such reversal. This line of analysis has a respectable ancestry, including Gluckman's (1963) classic theory of symbolic status reversal in rigidly hierarchical societies and Bateson's (1958) treatment of transvestite performances as "negative feedback" to a social system marked by polarized male/female personality models.

This volume's celebrations are replete with inversion and license. The Mount Forest festival begins with a costume ball in which the citizenry disguise and negate their personal identities, and moves later to a pyjama-dance in which hierarchy is replaced with egalitarianism, and social distance with warmth and camaraderie. The two festivals in Minnesota are periods of unaccustomed permissiveness regarding public drinking, pranks, and sexual display,[3] although in Glenwood such behavior is challenged by those who insist on projecting Waterama as sanitized "family entertainment." Professional wrestling is a dramatized violation of law, order, and justice, the cornerstone of North American civics. Festival gambling in Bermuda constructs a scenario of black wealth and power that is nonexistent in the actual political economy, and further flaunts the norms of a culture strongly influenced by evangelical Protestantism. The Rio *Carnaval* is given over to *fantasia*, the term appropriately chosen for the creative masks and costumes of the *sambistas*; it is a time when authority structures and behavioral norms are upended, and when adults assume the faculties of children. The child masqueraders in Sierra Leone reverse the normal relationship between themselves and their parents, and flagrantly attack images of the adult world. The two cowboy festivals glamorize an ideology that is contradicted by historical fact. The powwow depicts a notion of Indian identity that contrasts radically with the existential condition of most North American Indians, including the powwow clientele. To appropriate Babcock's phrase, then, all of our celebrations work semantically to "render the discrete both indiscrete and indiscreet" (1978:26).

But just as celebration reverses and violates ordinary reality, it also replicates and upholds it. There is a radical contrast *within* celebration, not just *between* celebration and the everyday world. In the Mount Forest festival, fantasy and *communitas* bracket a dramatic presentation of the community's exclusiveness and power structure. In Minnesota, each town festival reflects and 'certifies' key aspects of community organization: dichotomized sex rules in Foley, corporate socioeconomic relations in Glenwood. In professional wrestling, the principles of democracy are disputed, but the actual experience of the underclass in democratic societies is confirmed; all too often, nice guys really do finish last. In the Bermudian gambling tent, the fantasy of a black millenium is set against a representation of white domination; the tent is fittingly named the stock market, an image of the economic world in which blacks are subordinate clients. The Rio *Carnaval,* although built on structural reversals, is on one basic level "... the reverse of fiction or fake: it demands validity of feeling...." Moreover, the Cariocas of Rio, like Trinidadians, New Orleanians, and other carnivalists, cherish an underlying view of themselves as cavalier hedonists whose essential ethos is revealed, not reversed, in their annual Dionysian celebration (Taylor 1982:301). In the Sierra Leone children's masquerade performance, the upending of authority relations and the undermining of adult values are challenged by the shit devil, who pokes fun at the other masqueraders as well as at the adult world; if conventional values are not exactly affirmed, the negation of them is at least viewed with jocular suspicion. In the Calgary Stampede, the myth of a cowboy identity is belied by the event's hard-sell commercialism, a trait consistently characteristic of Calgary's actual history. In the Saskatchewan powwow, cultural pride and social solidarity are offset by a rather naked form of political maneuvering that the Indians themselves experience and expect in those who act as brokers between them and white society. What we see, then, is that celebration is cosmos as well as chaos, an authentic account of social reality as much as a deliberate disfigurement of it. Celebration's relationship to the normative social order involves, in Duvignaud's apt phrase, "transgression and consummation" (1976:14).

The dramatization of affirmation and negation has been insightfully discussed by Handelman (1977) under the headings of play and ritual. Play, he contends, bears the message "Let us make believe." It is a metastatement of pretense. It delivers an amoral commentary on society, an understanding of what can be. Ritual lies at an opposite epistemological pole, with the message "Let us believe." It is a metastatement of truth, delivering a moral critique of society, an understanding of what ought to be.

Handelman contends that play and ritual are the principle modes of liminality in traditional cultures and serve as a performative counterpoint to the contradiction between a society's actualities and its ideals. The connection between the two modes is complementary as well as contrastive. "The experience of play can prepare one for ritual, and that of ritual for play" (1977:188). Handelman emphasizes—and this is the major heuristic contribution of his essay—that it is the dramatic sequencing of play and ritual that warrants further investigation, not the relationship of either to the social context.

In contemporary cultures—those whose performance genres we might term, following Turner (1977), "liminoid" rather than "liminal"—the issue is more complex. Modernization's central ideological thrust has undermined the logical and performative complementarity of play and ritual. Ludic pretense is viewed as an impediment, not an enhancement, to truth and serious purpose. In considering contemporary celebrations, it is therefore essential to analyze not only the juxtaposition of the play/pretense and ritual/truth modes, but also their relationship, singly and together, to modernity.

As Weber (1958) realized, Reformation Protestantism was a crucial stimulus in the modernization of Western societies. Protestantism's major influence was to rationalize action and thought, a moral thrust that exalted relentless asceticism and methodical, productive work and that also refocused religious expression from liturgical elaboration to literal study of the Bible, deemed the only source of truth. The social results of this ethic, which gradually became secularized, are seen both in the utilitarian basis of modern capitalism—the point underscored by Weber—and in the modern tendency to value "realism" and "reason," while placing a pejorative connotation on "fantasy," "imagination," "myth," and other terms denoting modes of consciousness beyond the scope of empirical verification (Cox 1969: 59-67). Play is no longer forbidden on moral grounds, as it was in the puritan Commonwealth, but is accepted less as an end in itself—Huizinga's (1955) criterion—than as a means toward other ends. Thus *professional* sport and the entertainment *business* have become major industries, and games are encouraged among youth because they are seen as building character and teaching skills.

Western social science, it should be pointed out, has also accepted these premises. The systematic study of play began only a generation ago (Schwartzman 1978: 5), and much of it has been done from a functionalist perspective. In addition, scholars of play have had to justify their subject by calling it "recreation," a term that identifies its role in revitalizing the body and mind for more serious and useful pursuits (Norbeck 1974: 36).

But Protestantism and its cultural descendants have not been alone in stifling play. Contemporary reformist Islam, which has been compared to early Protestantism as a modernizing influence (Geertz 1960: 121-225; Peacock 1978a), has had similar effects. Dealing with Indonesia, Peacock (1978b) has shown that clowns and transvestites, ludic figures of inversion and license who occupy a central place in dramatic traditions, have been among the chief targets of Islamic reform groups. The specific opposition stems from religious morality, but he suggests a broader principle based on the difference between the "classificatory" logic of traditional societies and the "instrumental" logic of modern and modernizing societies:

> The classificatory world view, which emphasizes the subsuming of symbols within a frame, nourishes and is nourished by symbols of reversal; the instrumental world view, which emphasizes the sequential harnessing of means to an end, threatens and is threatened by such symbols. The instrumental world view would reduce all forms to mere means toward the ultimate end, but symbols of reversal call forth enchantment with the form and veneration of the cosmic categories it embodies, a fixation dangerous to the forward movement, the struggle [toward modernization]... (1978b: 221-22).

In its strict Calvinistic form, Protestantism abhorred ritual as much as play, construing the former as irrational magic and the latter as time-wasting and dangerously seductive. In contemporary and more popular forms, however, Protestantism has accommodated to, and in fact actively promoted, the chief secular variant of ritual: public ceremony (Fox 1980: 53). Ceremonial celebrations, for example, are the major rituals of America's Protestant-oriented "civil religion" (Bellah 1967; Warner 1953). Elaborating this perspective, Grimes (1976) has observed that the organized, uniformed, parade—a quintessential expression of social structure and idealized values—is the major symbolic movement through space in Protestant cultures, easily distinguished from the ludic masquerade and mummering parades that highlight the festivities of blacks and ethnic Catholics (Edmonson 1956;

Welch 1970). What Apter (1965: 266-356) calls "political religions"—highly moralistic ideologies that envision modernization as a kind of secular salvation—also tend to favor rite and ceremony over play, as witnessed by the profusion throughout the developing world of military parades, state shrines, political pageantry, and ritualistic public meetings aimed at "explaining" government ideology to the populace (Moore and Myerhoff 1977).

Regarding the celebrations discussed in this volume, it is apparent that although play and ritual are discernible in all cases, there is an imbalance, often radical, between the two modes. Where Protestant cultural influences predominate, the playful mode is muted and the ritual mode emphasized. The Glenwood Waterama is consciously conceived as a testimony to this Lutheran town's social structure and modern-oriented value system, and in these respects contrasts vividly with Fun Days in the more traditional Catholic town of Foley. The Mount Forest and Calgary celebrations sanctify an official ideology and foreclose alternate perspectives on society. In Mount Forest the only challenge to orthodoxy comes from the clown-like group from another town who have been invited to provide a bit of comic relief. In the Calgary Stampede, clowning is restricted to slapstick farce. Konrad reports that many newspeople privately refer to the event as the "stupede," but continue to file laudatory copy about it. He continues:

> One knocks the Stampede at one's own risk. Its myths about the past, the wildness of the stock used, the city's wildwest heritage, its fantastic international reputation, the intrinsic Calgaryness of the white hat symbol, the total acceptance and participation of community members— these items are accepted, perpetuated, and treated with great dignity rather than analyzed or critically evaluated.

Ideological control is so complete that the Stampede Board has hired its own publicity agent to conduct an evaluation of the festival.

The prevalence of ritualistic celebrations in modern societies evokes again MacCannell's (1976) interesting theory. He contends that modern cultural productions are centrally preoccupied with authenticity. As the modern world itself is seen as shallow and spurious, our most popular cultural productions (which, *inter alia,* are typically tourist attractions) are based on themes drawn from other cultures, or, more likely, from the historical past. In either case the social imagery is redolent with simplicity, truth, naturalness, and purity, qualities that are amply evidenced in our essays on community festivals, the Calgary Stampede, and Indian powwow. The combined emphasis of cultural productions on authenticity and history (or "heritage," as in some of our cases) constitutes an important part of "the conquering spirit of modernity—the grounds of its unifying consciousness" (MacConnell 1976:3). Modern peoples seek authenticity even in cultural productions which, in their own performance context, represent deliberate pretense. For example, North American tourists are likely to go to *Carnaval* in Rio not to revel in *fantasia,* but to encounter a pristine and genuine spirit of festivity that they believe has been "lost" in their own society. Perhaps this is why, as Turner suggests in this volume, so many of today's tourists are "closet pilgrims."

Alternately, the less modern Caribbean, Latin American, and African celebrations give much greater "play" to inversion, license, and other ludic tropes. The Bermudian stock market reveals the power structure of race relations, but its expressive thrust is to mask and transform that reality through symbols that associate blackness with money. The mock bullfight in Copal has intentional ideological significance, but it is carnivalesque in the traditional Catholic (and etymological) sense, a period of indulgence that is set in juxtaposition, temporally and spatially, to a period of ascetic religious observance. The bullfight reverses the morality, if not the underlying objective, of the church services that precede and follow it; playful, pantomimed fighting is performed as an 'interlude' to serious prayer and rigorous devotions. The Rio *Carnaval* (this time, from the Carioca's perspective) is play *par excellence,* an archetypal illustration of the human capacity for multilevelled ludic expression. As Turner contends, "All Caillois' components are sparking away furiously at once, like the plugs in a racing car or the wheels of Ezekial's chariot." The Sierra Leone masquerade upends and lampoons the power structure at the same time that it pokes fun at itself. The shit devil is a kind of double negative, a satirical inversion of a satirical inversion, just as the communication between child performers and adult audience is built on a double joke.

Symbolism and Politics

If we examine further the symbolism of the play and ritual modes of celebration, we can better consider the question of their political implications and functions. Celebratory play has a metaphoric structure and content. Its dominant symbols, costumes and clowns, convey a sense of the *mundus inversus* by transforming ordinary reality into an alternate domain of symbolic discourse. Ludic celebrations often present what Babcock (1973: 25-29) calls a "surplus of signifiers," a kind of sensory overload created by a Rabelaisian profusion of images and intermingled categories. Hence their semantics are open-ended, unorthodox, fragmented, and often highly individualized, enabling them to elude control and to transcend or subvert ideology.

In contrast, celebratory ritual is essentially metonymical. It communicates meaning through the principle that Turner (1967: 54) calls *pars pro toto*; a limited number of highly condensed forms represent and integrate a wide spectrum of cultural data. Its dominant symbols—uniforms, flags, other emblems of ideology and social structure—are what Ortner (1973) terms "summarizing" symbols; they affirm, unify, and soberly reinforce a broad field of conceptual and emotional significance. Ritualistic celebration thus conveys a version of the social order that is meant to be believed, or at least acknowledged and adhered to, and over which society exerts control.

The political significance of metaphor and metonymy has been discussed by Paine (1981: 187-200). Whereas his field of reference is the rhetorical performance of politicians, the argument is equally valid when applied to celebratory performance. Metaphor, he proposes, works to promote change. It extends meaning, relates one form of comprehension to another, and supports the suitability of alternate interpretations and responses. Accordingly, metaphor flourishes among those who are relatively powerless, and whose pragmatic interests lie in changing the balance in their favor. Contrastingly, metonymy works to retard change. It reduces and restricts thought to the familiar, containing it within images and experiences that are already known. Its structure is closed, and virtually tautological. It therefore flourishes among those who are relatively powerful, and whose interests lie in maintaining the status quo.

This argument is clearly consistent with our ethnography. Ludic and metaphorical celebrations enjoy their greatest vitality among those who are marginal not only to the cultural mainstream of modernization, but also to political power: the blacks of Bermuda, the slum dwellers of Rio, the children of Sierra Leone, and the Mayan villagers of Yucatan. Alternately, it is among those in quite the opposite political and cultural position—the Calgary establishment, leading business and political figures in "successful" towns like Mount Forest and Glenwood—that ritualistic and metonymical modes of celebration are more highly valued.

But this perspective must be seen in relation to another. While the logic of celebration is ideological and structural, the process of celebration is competitive and dialectical. As a public and participatory phenomenon, celebration is unusually open to conflicting claims. Social rivals contend for power, prestige, and other objectives within the context of celebration as well as beyond it. Like other cultural productions, therefore, celebration does not simply "reflect" the political field. It is integrally, and influentially, part of it.

This line of thought has been developed by Cohen (1974), whose influence is amply evident in this volume. "Political Man," he indicates, "is also Symbolist Man" (1974:v). There is an ongoing dialectical or "two-dimensional" dynamic connection between symbolic expression and power relations, each responsive to the other. Cohen (1982) extends this notion in a discussion of how symbolic events are "contested" by sociopolitical opponents. Generalizing from his own study of Britain's Notting Hill Carnival to the carnival genre, he discusses

> ...the potentialities of carnival for articulating both hegemonous and opposition political formations. Both orientations are present in every carnival, thus in effect posing a contradiction within a unity of form. Like a grand joking relationship, carnival expresses both alliance and enmity, both consensus and conflict, at one and the same time. In other words, it is an ambiguous symbolic

formation that camouflages and mystifies a contradiction (1982:37).

Continuing, he contends that ideally there is an even balance between the two forms of expression. Were the balance to be radically disturbed, carnival would be transformed into a different genre:

> If the festival is made to express pure and naked hegemony, it becomes a massive political rally of the type staged under totalitarian political systems. On the other hand, if it is made to express pure opposition, it becomes a political demonstration against the system. In either extreme case it ceases to be a carnival (1982:37).[4]

Thus, although celebration remains in continuing flux, there is always likely to be a duality, however asymmetrical, between progressive and conservative forces, between the competitive strengths of relatively powerless social elements and their relatively powerful opponents. In this volume that tension is examined in the discussion of Foley Fun Days and the Copal fiesta, and there are allusions to it elsewhere.

Our examples further reveal that celebration not only represents, but also promotes, dynamic political processes, including the realignment of forces and interests within the body politic. Sometimes, as in the cases of the Parklund Powwow, and, to a lesser extent, the Calgary Stampede, a celebration reaches a stage where the political objectives of those who control it are essentially realized, and it therefore declines. Alternately, a celebration at that stage "changes hands," with appropriate changes in content form, and significance—a situation that appears to be emerging in Foley.

In our other key, there is a duality, not necessarily balanced, between play and ritual. Whereas modernity and hierarchy push celebration in the direction of ritual, the ludic capacity of celebration, aided often by those who cling to traditional and populist orientations, tends to push back. To evoke Cohen's observation in support of a parallel position, if celebration moved too far in the direction of ritualism, it would be reduced to literalism and utilitarianism, shedding not only its ludic qualities but also its liminoid identity. Equally, if celebration moved too far in the direction of play, it would become mere escapism, void of a meaningful relationship with the actual experience of the celebrants.

The coincidence of opposites, then, lies at the heart of celebration's symbolic and political vitality. Celebration does not resolve or remove ambiguity and conflict, but embellishes them. It locates these basic and eternal social facts, as Durkheim might have called them, in a performance context in which they can be thought about, acted upon, and aesthetically appreciated. The celebrant's hope, as our epigraph suggests, is that the rhythm of performance will find an echo in life, if only for the moment.

Notes

I am grateful to Dennis Duerden, Ronald Grimes, Jean-Marc Philibert, and all of the volume's contributors for their comments on an earlier draft of this introductory essay.

[1]The term "modern" is used here in a general Weberian sense to indicate the dominance of rationality over custom as a principle and method of social organization. From this perspective, the classificatory characteristics of modernity include bureaucracy, centralization, universalism, secularism, and so on, as well as industrial, technological and urban development. For an extended discussion of these features see Levy (1965).

[2]As I write this, the television series M*A*S*H has just shown its final program. Throughout the city of London, Ontario—in hotels, bars, restaurants—fans of the series came together to watch the last episode on large screens. They dressed as M*A*S*H characters, and ate military communal dinners of franks and beans. News reports indicated that strangers became emotional companions as they shared laughter and tears together.

[3]This information comes primarily from one of Lavenda's students, Mark Laver, who did much of the fieldwork in Foley. His findings were given in a report presented at the 1982 meeting of the Association for the Anthropological Study of Play in London, Ontario.

[4]These are not simply hypothetical possibilities. In Cuba, the Castro regime rescheduled *Carnaval* from pre-Lent to July, in order to strip the festival of its traditional religious significance and to make it instead a ritualized commemoration of the Castro revolution, which began in July.

Part II

Community Festivals

Chapter 2

High, Healthy and Happy: Ontario Mythology on Parade

Carole Farber

> Ethnology is not a speciality defined by a particular subject, 'primitive societies.' It is a way of thinking, the way which imposes itself when the subject is 'different' and requires us to transform ourselves. We also become ethnologists of our own society if we set outselves at a distance from it.... This is a remarkable method, which consists in learning to see what is ours as alien and what was alien as our own.... At the point where two cultures cross, truth and error dwell together, either because our own training hides what there is to know from us, or on the contrary because it becomes, in our life in the field, a means of incorporating other people's differences.
>
> Maurice Merleau-Ponty *Signs* (1964: 120)

Festivals, mass spectacles, and other cultural performances have received recent attention from anthropologists and ethnologists, especially from those who identify themselves as 'symbolic anthropologists' (cf. Babcock 1978; Basso and Selby 1976; Singer 1972; Turner 1967, 1974a, 1978b). However, these symbolic and performative phenomena have been of interest to folklorists, sociologists, popular culturists and historians, for a longer period of time (cf. Dorson 1972; Orgel 1975; Warner 1959). It is clear from all of these sources that cultural performances provide ideal *entrees* into a community's symbolic, economic, social, and political life, especially because they are organized and presented to members of the community by members of the community. Cultural performances are also meant for "outsiders" to get the message of the community, as evidenced by the encouragement given to me to witness and participate in the festivities discussed in this paper.

Warner (1959), Singer (1972, 1977) and Grimes (1976) have written the most on North American community festivals, each from a different point of view. In all cases, however, it is apparent that festivals are about identity, whether personal or social, and they are the context and the process of creating links between people in the community, as well as between the community and the wider national and cultural environment. The importance of history and its enactment and re-enactment in the present seems to be an especially important element. Grimes examines the Santa Fe public celebrations in terms of how they transact the historical relationship between various ethnic elements in the population; Warner discusses Yankee City public activities in terms of how they create and sustain the meaning of direct links with American founding communities; and Singer, in a re-analysis of Warner's work (albeit from a predominantly psychological perspective), analyses the creation and maintenance of metalinks with the American tradition. Each emphasizes, nonetheless, that the creation of identity links through a festival, itself an event that is limited to the here and now in time and space, expresses the nexus between public symbolism and politics (Cohen 1974).

It is this public aspect of festivity, its transformation and performance of official town ideology and myth, that I intend to explicate in this paper. Town ideologies and myths provide a context of interpretation for insiders and outsiders alike. Mythological forms "are the forms of representation that 'naturalize' certain meanings ... (Barthes quoted in Coward and Ellis 1977: 26). Official public myths—those generated, espoused and supported by the people who control public images and public activity—are a specific variety of myth that sustains a sense of identity and continuity for a large segment of the population who come in contact with them. It is in the official public myths that we can see the "symbolic order and the power order ... involved in the creation and recreation of selfhood and also in the dynamics of continuity and change" (Cohen 1974: 138). Cohen suggests further that the relationship between the two orders "can be found in the search for, and analysis of, key dramatic performances..." p. 132). In what

The town of Mount Forest celebrates itself—the past paraded in the present

follows I am arguing that the small-town summer festival is precisely one of these key dramatic performances—a performance in which official town myths and ideology are presented and re-presented in parades, talent shows, costume judging, sports competitions, masquerades, and the like.

Central to the ideological structure of most Canadian communities is the consideration of history or 'heritage.' This can be seen in the increasing number of festivals that are celebrations of the lifestyle and virtues of the past. In Ontario alone, over 400 summer festivals are devoted to the past (a large number have a rural or ethnic flavor, as well). Ever since the Canadian centennial celebrations in 1967, the past has become even more important in the Canadian present. Government grants in support of community celebrations have increased, as has the involvement of corporations.

This paper focuses on Old Home Week in Mount Forest, Ontario, an event which has been enacted approximately every ten years since the turn of the century. I will first describe the town, then analyse the festival in temporal and spatial terms, and finally interpret the parade as a statement to insiders and outsiders of the official links within and between communities. I view the festival as a kind of public manifesto, suggesting that it can be read as a text, either as a narrative or documentary (Ricoeur 1971; Geertz 1972) that articulates and celebrates the town's political economy and underlying mythology.

The Town as Context

The residents of Mount Forest have always been proud of the economic, political, social, patriotic, and traditional public face of the community. Beginning with the earliest collected written statements about Mount Forest (Wright 1927) to the written and verbal portrayals by current and former residents in 1977, Mount Forest has been presented as a stable, viable, and nationally committed community, with an idealized image of harmony and good Canadian virtues and traditions. As written in the Canadian centennial edition of the local newspaper, *The Confederate,*

> Indeed, all good things in life seem to be kept well in hand
> by the service clubs, fraternal orders, Legion Auxiliaries,

Institutes, clubs and almost all sports and recreation facilities. Our town is truly beautiful with its many parks. Its citizens take great pride in their trees, gardens, lawns, and shrubs. Our commercial enterprises serve well and our rural community shares with us both the work and the benefits of our good life. I do not know who composed our motto, but we live it well: HIGH, HEALTHY, AND HAPPY.

The town of Mount Forest currently supports a population of 3,400. Located in the northernmost tip of Wellington County, it is surrounded by glens and forests, fields and pastures, and the Saugeen River. The largest town in a 30-mile radius, it serves and services a rural and urban population of about 15,000. The town has become a manufacturing center (since the original study, another large industry has announced location in Mount Forest), as well as a commercial, social service center for the surrounding five or six townships. Many residents told me, with some pride, that "people come here to shop all the way from Guelph" (a larger center approximately 40 miles away). The public media, as well as residents, are eager to quote production and revenue figures of the town in demonstration of the prosperity of the community.[1] In 1977 there were some 103 businesses lined up along Main Street and 10 more businesses scattered around the periphery. Lists of the names and owners of these businesses are an important part of the official town publications.

Until 1965 the manufacturing businesses in Mount Forest were involved in the transformation of natural products: milk and milk products, lumber and wood products, gravel products, aerated water, and animals and leather products—all resources available in the area surrounding the town. Until 1970 or so, nearly all of the retail stores were locally owned or franchised to local residents; they were frequently family businesses, and often united several prominent families. By the time of research, however, there were some synthetic manufacturing plants making plastic adhesive emblems, and some of the retail stores were owned by people outside the immediate locale—some from as far away as Toronto and the United States. Branch plants and foreign ownership had arrived in Mount Forest—a trend that is continuing in the 1980s.

In addition, the town is surrounded by reasonably fertile agricultural lands and productive livestock pens. The natural products from these sources are corn, beans and small grains, beef and pork, as well as timber. Cattle are raised for both milk and meat, and the countryside is laced with cheese factories.

The organization of the town itself is typical of southwestern Ontario towns. The formal power structure is the elected mayor and council, reeve and deputy reeve, clerks and service personnel. In looking over the lists of office-holders for the past 15 years, it is apparent that leadership is drawn from a fairly narrow circle, with many people holding the same office for several years and/or people holding the same offices over the years. There is an interesting, though not at all surprising, communication between town leadership and business ownership. Many of the town councillors own businesses that are prosperous, or are partners in some of the more viable revenue and employment-generating firms.

Mount Forest has a number of voluntary associations. There are service clubs, sports clubs, religious institutions, educational organizations, and patriotic associations. These groups divide the population into various discrete units with overlapping memberships, each with its own rules and rights (rites) of identification. Most of the major church denominations and sects are represented—United Church, Anglican, Presbyterian, Catholic (with both a church and a school), Pentecostal, Baptist, and Lutheran. Each of these religious bodies sponsors service and social agencies for youth, men, and women. The Presbyterian, United, Anglican, and Catholic churches rank above the others in terms of their community and regional economic and political prominence. In addition to the church organizations, youth groups such as Guides and Boy Scouts are present, as are the voluntary associations of Kinsmen, Optimists, and Lions and the fraternal organizations of Masons and Rebekahs. The economic organizations, the Agricultural Society (which runs the fall fair) and the Businessmen's Association, also occupy a central position in the community. Mount Forest, then, is a typical small town.

I turn now to the summer decennial festival, Old Home Week. This is an intentionally symbolic occurrence that is a reunion in at least two senses: it is a large family gathering and a re-union of town goals and aims with a public celebration of official myths and town ideology.

Old Home Week

In the Old Home Week celebration, Mount Forest is presented as a vibrant, unified, good and natural symbol, both at the time of the festival and as it is thought of and written about in retrospect. Former resident Kenneth Smith wrote the following of his experience:

> ... a word of commendation for the planners and organisers of the four-day event which so appropriately centred around the institutions and organizations that give the town its real strength—the churches, the schools, the service clubs, and other community groups. It was a strong reminder of the fact that in a rapidly urbanizing Canada the essential character of the country is still exemplified in small town life, more effectively than in metropolitan centers (Mount Forest *Confederate,* 13 July 1977).

His was typical of the responses in the newspapers that followed the celebration. They all stressed the importance of a rural or small community, the interrelatedness of the agencies in the community, and the public and positive values they embodied. The activities and festivities of Old Home Week occupied most of the residents physically and mentally, most of the time before and during the event. There was a great deal of emphasis on rural/urban solidarity and on the fairness and openness of the community, both in organizing the festival and in playing it out. In the words of the chairwoman of the Entertainment Committee, this festival is one where "There's going to be something for everybody and everybody is going to be doing something" (Mount Forest *Confederate,* 11 May, 1977). The main message of Old Home Week for most of the celebrants was Community Solidarity, Community Continuity, and Community Equality, involving all people— former, current and neighboring residents alike.

Looking more closely at the planning, structure and sequence of Old Home Week makes it evident that this festival is a microcosm of the agencies that provide the definition of public activity for this community. If it is taken as a whole, the planning and execution of the various publicized events of the festival, Old Home Week can be seen as the presentation and performance of shared meanings—a symbolic re-presentation of the asserted, believed and controlled community identity.

The festival involved, at the organizational level, a large number of local residents, forming 17 committees whose leadership and volunteer committee workers represented more than 100 townspeople. Even though the committee leadership was predictable (from the narrow circle outlined above), some of the committee workers were not defined public personnel; some were volunteers who were otherwise not involved in many public activities. At the celebration and public-witnessing level, an estimated 8,000 people were involved (the town population is about 3,400 people). This festival was woven from the cooperative effort of many people—people willing to expend their time and energy sustaining the links with one another, with former residents and the neighboring residents, and with the official town mythology. Whether for current, former or neighboring residents, Old Home Week served as a public unifying statement—a metacommunity assertion. In the words of the overall organizer of Old Home Week:

> There is something special—almost sacred—about coming home. As we grow older the impact of passing time becomes greater. For former residents Old Home Week means a return to the town they once lived in. It gives a chance for them, and for all of us, to again visit childhood scenes and to renew old friendships (Mount Forest *Confederate,* 29 June 1977).

The leadership of the planning committees was drawn from locally prominent educational, religious, economic and political personnel, all of whom were concerned that a united and vital public face be presented to all participants; a public face that consciously linked the past with the present, the rural with the urban, and the good, true and stable with them both. Occasional meetings of committee personnel with the chairman of the festival were intended to ensure that the events would run smoothly and without complications.

The festival agenda was as follows:

1st day: School visitations, Church garden party, Costume Ball and Costume Judging.
2nd day: 'Monster' or 'Mammoth' Parade, Concerts and Performance

by parade participants, Sports competition, Beard Judging and CKNX Barn Dance.
3rd day: Church Services, Sports Competitions, Pyjama Parade.
4th day: Legion Activities and dedication, Sports Competition, Community Sing and Bonfire.

In interpreting the festival as a whole, it is important to notice the sequence of events.In this way, the festival can be analysed as a key dramatic event or a performance of town ideology and myth. This dramatic enactment resembles a *rite de passage* (cf. Leach 1961; Turner 1967), but with a difference; it is a symbolic re-enactment of the rites of passage that are crucial in the events that inform Mount Forest and Canadian values. Taken as a kind of lineal narrative (Peacock 1969) that leads participants through their life experiences, the festival begins with an emphasis on education and the secular and religious agencies responsible for it, moves on to the costume ball where people "become what they are not" and on to the second and third days, when they celebrate "who they are" morally, secularly and publicly. Who they are, is presented in a few events of parading, competing, and dancing. Once that sequence has been established as the Official Town View, they can invert that view and assert another Official Town View of equality and humoresque. This leads people to the end of the festival where the links to the nation are enacted.

The spatial dimensions of the festival and the structural position of events can be seen as presenting and representing the boundaries and limits of community involvement. The edges or the outer rims of the festival show the agencies that tie locals into the national scene—the educational agencies and the patriotic agencies—the outside in general. These are in juxtaposition to the inside—the agencies that tie local and surrounding areas together. The outside prepares one for life in Canadian society; the inside celebrates what it means to be an insider in this community.

It is the inside—the parades, sports competitions, barn dance, local church services, and so on—that typify the official community myth, the one that is ritualized and dramatized. Typical of the events on the inside, and I argue, central to the meaning of the festival as a whole, are the oppositionally placed parades. The meaning of the social forms, such as parades, ties in their publicness, their assertions about what is to be seen. The social and cultural practice of parading, in addition to making temporal and spatial links of the present with the past, provides a kind of meta social commentary.

Parading the Past, the Stable and the Natural

In the often-neglected work on an American community called "Yankee City," Lloyd Warner provides a systematic, imaginative, and inspirational symbolic analysis of the town's meaningful public life. Volume V of this work, entitled *The Living and the Dead*, deals specifically with the kind of public statements that emphasize the importance of the past. Warner makes a statement that I would like to use as a point of departure, and later modify:

> An activity such as a parade or an installation of officers is recognized and socially defined as public use of symbols in a set of formal or informal social relations. An activity is recognized as such by those who participate in it and by those who study it at the explicit and open level of behavior. Each activity occurs in a situation which involves the relations of the members alone, or the members of the community. Each activity includes a symbolic situation in which members exchange symbols among themselves or with other members of the society according to the nature of the relations (Warner 1959: 235).

Before proceeding to the performance of the parades, we must, as Warner underscores, consider the relations and the social organization of the production of the parades, which demonstrate some of the political and economic forces of the town working together.

The parade committee was headed by the mayor himself (who is also a prominent businessman), and he was assisted by four other businessmen and their wives; hence, the organization of the parade was a family enterprise. This committee processed the entry forms for those volunteering to parade, and also solicited the participation of groups outside Mount Forest—such as bands, floats, and the like. They also arranged the parade entries in an order that blended the various musical, historical, and civic entries in such a way as to keep the interest of everyone. The parade committee also acted as judges for the entries in the different categories

The Cameron highlanders in full dress

(outlined later), and as the focal point for a large number of questions and inquiries about the composition of various entries.

The Mammoth Parade, the main parade of the festival, was definitely a display of the symbols of community organization and tradition; it was a parade of the various community groups and "the performance of past activities and places." The route of the parade covered the entire length of Main Street (blocking through-province traffic)—to be seen by all—a lineal re-creation and public use of shared values. After a pre-parade procession of some 50 antique and old-model cars, the parade proper began, led by the Mount Forest Cameron Pipers, the local lottery-supported (Wintario) pipe band. Through the entries that followed, the town, the surrounding areas, and their relationships to one another unfolded publicly. There were a variety of entries, summarized as follows: 13 floats, either business or club-sponsored; 13 rural entries, including horses; 11 firetrucks from Mount Forest and surrounding towns; 4 sports clubs; 4 service clubs; 3 school entries; 2 religious entries; 2 patriotic clubs; as well as costume winners, children's entries, and the like. The parade had over 90 entries and lasted one hour—clearly a fast and compressed enactment.

Just as the political and economic forces controlled the organizational level, they were prominently displayed in the parade itself. Many of the downtown businesses and peripheral businesses had float entries, or they donated their trucks, complete with business name or insignia, as flat-cars or towing vehicles for other community entries. The business presence accounted for almost one half of the entries, and ranged from several Canada Packers trucks to the lumber and construction company trucks that were donated for the use of entrants such as the Mount Forest Old Brass Band or the Girls' Softball League winners.

Equally as revealing was the absence of a few major Mount Forest employers and economic forces in the parade performance. Why should some of these industries and businesses be missing? These absences gave me an important clue for discovering what this whole festival was about and what it meant. Realizing that *Mac-Tac Mount Forest* and *K-Brand Mount Forest* were not represented made me see that the official myth or history being enacted in the parade was a selective one. A local resident informed me that both firms sponsor school floats for the December Santa Claus parade in Mount Forest[2]—a commercial event that involves most school-age Mount Forestians.

In order to interpret their absence and obtain a better insight into what Old Home Week is about, I will return to a distinction I made earlier between "real" insiders (natural businesses) and the "newcomers" (the synthetic businesses). Old Home Week is a symbolic and behavioral complex that is devoted to providing a medium for making statements, for both residents and nonresidents alike, about the continuing and official myth of community solidarity; the parade, in particular, is about parading the natural, the true and the stable. The newcomers and the synthetic businesses do not fit in; they say nothing that contributes to the official and intended meaning. In this case the newcomers and the synthetic businesses are the same people—a double dose of not belonging in the parade of the natural past to the present. An interesting test case of this observation is the presence of one newcomer business in the parade, *Acme Ruler Company*; this company only has a single outsider characteristic, since the business uses natural products in manufacturing rulers, cribbage boards, and the like. This business fits in with older businesses in town, and so can be present in the parade.

All the other entries—church, school, fraternal organizations—contributed to the meaning, and they did so by publicly performing as discrete groups of Mount Forestians, together, as Warner has said, in a "symbolic situation in which members exchange symbols among themselves or with other members of the society. . . ." The presence of the "institutions and organizations that give the town its real strength," and the themes and symbols they displayed in their entries publicly demonstrated "Our Good Old Home" through floats depicting either former buildings or pioneer and rural practices. The parade was the present as past or the present in historical and traditional tableau—captured in time for all to see.

The awards for the entries in the main parade are additional important clues as to what the festival is about, another public statement about the meaning of 'insider' and 'real' as opposed to 'outsider' and 'not real.' All the prizes, save

Comic commentary from outsiders enlivens Old Home Week in Mount Forest

one, were given to local groups, displaying the past, or at least the traditional. These were as follows:

Best Patriotic Float: The Mount Forest Old Home Week Float, pulled by the Reeves Construction (mayor related).
Best Historic Float: Mount Forest Kinsmen.
Best Theme: Woodland UCW showing butter churning and quilt making.
Best Commercial Entry: Carpet Country (carpets and clowns).
Best School Entry: Mount Forest Public School.
Best Service Club: Rebekah Lodge.
Best Decorated Bicycle: Mike and Chris Peach.

As is probably evident, both the category of winners and the actual winners are important in this parade. History, patriotism, and community involvement are important in parading the present as the past, good, stable, and true. The Carpet Country winning requires some explanation. Although this business is a rather new one in Mount Forest, it is a prosperous retail outlet, run by an old Mount Forest family, and so it is less inappropriate than it may seem that they received an award in the commercial category.

There was one additional prize, which went to an outsider entry—the Hillbillies from Listowel (a town of about 5,000 people some 30 miles from Mount Forest). This entry is rich in symbolism and deserves more attention than I will give it here. It is a burlesque entry, exaggerating sexuality and bumpkiness. I suggest that in a parade that displays the official 'insiders' myth, outsiders, rather than locals, were the most appropriate ones to express the comic; the Listowel Hillbillies won the Most Humorous category. Some local residents entered humorous floats, but were regarded as less appropriate in the category. Other entries from the outside included bands, agricultural entries and fire trucks.

This Mammoth or Monster parade, then, was the official message of Old Home Week enacted. The official myth as controlled by those in positions of power is one that emphasizes the 'naturalness' of the past and the community political economy.

Sequentially, just as the placement of the costume ball led people into the official symbolic statement of the town, there

was a pyjama parade that led people back to their relationships
of equality as members of the community and the Canadian
public in general. This parade provides a number of direct
oppositions to the main parade. Instead of being held in
daylight, for all to see, this parade was held under the cover of
darkness; instead of parading through the main street and the
most public parts of town, it began at the edge of town, crossed
the main street and proceeded to the community arena where it
dissolved into a dance, everyone dancing in his/her pyjamas;
instead of the theme of the present as the past, this parade
displayed the present as the present, laid bare by the pyjama
symbolism, along with a minimum of make-up and props.
Nonetheless, the parade left an impression of masquerade. The
statement being made here, where everyone, including the
Mount Forest Cameron Pipers and town officials were levelled,
was, as one local resident told me, "that in your pyjamas we are
all the same."

   The pyjama parade was smaller than the daylight parade,
and there were fewer watchers but more direct participants. It
took place at midnight, yet carried an overt message. The
message was almost the inversion of what goes on in everyday
life in a small town where political and economic control are as
concentrated as they are in Mount Forest; the message paraded
the official myth of equality. Rather than emphasizing
temporal links, as the main parade did, the pyjama parade
emphasized spatial and interactional links between
community members. The pyjama parade of equality led the
people not to the past but to the next day's events, which
demonstrated how all Canadians should be patriotic and
bound to their community.

   In these parades, residents, former residents and members
of neighboring communities engaged in a public ideological
practice that had binding and compelling qualities. As Warner
says:

> When members of a society assign meaning to themselves,
> things, and their own activities, they are acting together
> (collectively participating in myths or creating history) ...
> [providing] a system of meaningful acts commonly shared.
> Paradoxically, although protean and changing in time
> and context, most meanings hold constant and
> unchanging (1959: 452).

Additional Meaning in Forms

> The practice of ideology has succeeded when it has
> produced [a] 'natural attitude'; when, for example, the
> existing relations of power are not only accepted but
> perceived precisely as the way things are, ought to be, and
> will be.
>
> (Coward and Ellis: 1977: 68)

I have tried to demonstrate how a cultural celebration unites public symbolism and political order. By getting 3,000 additional people to participate in recognizing the value of Mount Forest (doubling the town's population for four days) the townsfolk made the following metastatement about themselves: (1) they still have purchase power on their former residents; (2) they have control both of themselves and the surrounding areas; (3) their values are natural, stable and true; and (4) they have the power to lead a celebration of this happy family reunion—Old Home Week.

The small town celebration that "has something for everybody and everybody doing something," demonstrates the values of the people who are concerned with community solidarity and community identity. As visiting Member of Parliament, Perrin Beatty, remarked about the festival:

> It was just great. Everyone said it was the best event of its
> kind they'd ever seen, and that says a great deal for the
> community spirit in Mount Forest. I think you'd be hard-
> pressed to find a city that could organize an event of this
> kind.... It takes a small town spirit to get so much
> volunteer effort coordinated.

I have hopefully shown that Old Home Week in Mount Forest gave the town a chance to live its motto—a community that is (for the public decennial festival, at least) HIGH, HEALTHY AND HAPPY.

Notes

The field study of Mount Forest took place in the summer of 1977, where I was teaching an introductory anthropology course. On the first day of classes I asked my students, "If I wanted to live easily and successfully in Mount Forest, what would I have to know and understand about the way things work here?" "Could I come to be an 'insider' here?" They collectively drew up lists of events, people and places that I should see and informed me about living in Mount Forest. One event was Old Home Week.

Although the interpretation of the data is my own, I would like to acknowledge the following for their help: Janice Cole, Dave Unger, the anthropology class in Mount Forest, and the symbolic anthropology class at the University of Western Ontario. I also thank Frederick Errington, Marjorie Halpin, and Frank E. Manning for their comments on earlier drafts of this paper.

[1]The value of manufactured goods in 1976-77 was over $4.5 million; the retail sales from local merchants and businesses exceeded $5 million in 1976-77; and there were numerous new buildings and some renovations of and additions to the service and sports facilities.

[2]It seems that it is appropriate for these synthetic businesses to support the new, or in this case the young of Mount Forest, as well as the commercial of Mount Forest, especially if they hope to become insiders at some future date.

Chapter 3

Family and Corporation: Two Styles of Celebration in Central Minnesota

Robert H. Lavenda

As winter relaxes its death grip on Minnesota and summer begins, the newcomer to the state cannot help being struck by the extraordinary number and variety of community festivals. One is struck, as well by the lengths to which people go to deny these festivals any significance other than "they're just for fun." This conjunction of near universality and the denial of importance should serve as a warning that there is, perhaps, more here than meets the eye.

This is especially true given the emerging literature on the importance to social life of festivals (Swiderski 1973; Ostor 1980; Grimes 1976; Buechler 1980) and carnivals (Manning 1978; DaMatta 1977a, 1977b; Lavenda 1980), much of it inspired by the work of Geertz (1972) and Turner (1974b, 1977). Following the approach of these latter scholars, in particular their emphasis on the text of such events—their reflexive, metasocial, metastructural nature—I wish to argue that one need not travel to Bali or Rio de Janeiro to encounter cultural texts. Closer-to-home festivals also provide people with a way of interpreting and shaping their experience of life. Geertz' caveat that "the culture of a people is an ensemble of texts, themselves ensembles," some of which qualify or challenge others (1972: 29) applies here as well: summer community festivals are not the only cultural texts in central Minnesota, but they are important ones, providing a base of common experience. However, they vary from community to community, providing different stories for different communities to tell themselves about themselves. By looking at two such texts, we may come to a better understanding of the social world of two communities in central Minnesota.

Two Towns, Two Festivals

The communities of Foley and Glenwood, Minnesota, provide striking contrasts in the textual quality of festivals. Foley, located in central Minnesota, some 15 miles from the city of St. Cloud, is a community of approximately 1,400 people, predominantly German and Polish Catholic. It is the seat of Benton County, serving a rural area of roughly 400 square miles. Until recently, Foley seemed to be a classic farm service town with banks, churches, bars, physicians, dentists, veterinary, drug stores, clothing stores, farm and dairy supply stores, grain elevators, implement and automobile dealers, and the like. In the past few years, however, some light industry has come to Foley, as has a large Land O' Lakes turkey hatchery. Additionally, today nearly a quarter of full-time workers living in Foley are employed in St. Cloud. Yet Foley retains a reputation in the surrounding areas of being a conservative, very inwardly directed community. Its festival, Fun Days, began in 1962. With the exception of one four-year period it has been organized by a single person, and has always remained a festival for Foley and its immediate area.

Glenwood is 75 miles west of Foley, on the shore of a large lake which attracts a sizeable number of cottagers and other summer vacationers. A local grocer underlined the significance of these seasonal residents when he noted that his business increases by 30 percent during the summer. Glenwood is larger than Foley, with some 2,600 residents, and is the seat of Pope County. Its mixed economy depends on tourism, the surrounding farm area, the railroad (Glenwood is a division point on the Soo Line), and on manufacturing, although this last has been something of a disappointment to the local development corporation.[1]

Glenwood is similar to Foley on the surface— a typical self-sufficient mid-western small town, composed of families that have lived there for generations, with businesses that have been in the same family for generations (cf. Martindale and

Hanson 1969: 16, 17 *passim*). In fact, however, Glenwood is an exception to this image. There are few businesses in Glenwood that have not been sold to newcomers at least once in the past 25 years. A Glenwood old-timer is someone who has been there for 15 years or more. The owner of the newspaper, who himself arrived in Glenwood 27 years ago from a small town in southwestern Minnesota, has had the opportunity to observe the remarkable amount of new typesetting that has been necessary every year to accommodate the population movement into and out of the community (the newspaper printed the telephone directory for many years). Despite this movement,, the town maintains an image of Scandinavian Lutheranism.

The Glenwood Waterama began in 1956, and has become the largest water-oriented festival in the state except those sponsored by the twin cities of Minneapolis and St. Paul. It attracts visitors from Iowa and the Dakotas, as well as from all over Minnesota. The festival, then, depends for its very survival on visitors from outside the area.

As can be seen from the above brief glance, these two rather different communities have different festivals. The difference is highlighted by their respective organizational styles.

Fun Days

Foley Fun Days, as noted above, has had one organizer for most of its existence. Officially under the control of the Foley Business Bureau, the actual organizer is the owner (along with her husband) of the local floral shop. She seeks volunteers to take charge of the various events of the festival, maintaining for herself the organization of a large parade and veto power over all other events. Her control can best be described as benevolent dictatorship: it is "her" festival. In 1976 she refused to organize the festival any longer, and control passed to the Jaycees. They, it is generally agreed, did not do a good job with it, and they eventually disbanded. The Business Bureau asked the former organizer to return, which she eventually did, but with the stipulation that she would have total control. Any attempt to thwart her would result in her immediate resignation.

There are two kinds of events associated with Fun Days, both of which affect the way the festival is organized. The first consists of those events which have become associated with the festival but which had a life of their own before it, or which came to the festival through a different organization. Thus, the Sportmen's Club Fish and Chicken Fry and the Softball Tournament, independently organized, have become incorporated into the festival. The second class of events are indigenous to the festival; that is, they originated with or came from suggestions to the organizer at the time Fun Days began. Examples include the queen pageant, the street sales, and the children's events.

What is striking about Fun Days is the way in which its organizational structure replicates the organization of traditional sex roles in Foley. The parade was organized by the female director but (ostensibly) supervised by men. Those activities which are traditionally male-oriented—softball tournament, trap-shooting, horseshoe tournament, Lucas tool demonstration, and fire department water fight—were organized by men, whereas those activities associated with the home—street sale, craft sale, arts and crafts, story hour, egg toss, and queen pageant—were organized by women. Indeed, the festival organizer justifies this division in terms of the natural order: "Women just seem to do much better with small children. And they have a natural aptitude for working with arts and crafts."

It is not in the organization alone that this division is concerned. It is also enacted every summer as community members participate differentially in the festival. Counts made at the events of the festival reveal that almost no events attract males and females equally. The queen pageant was attended by three times as many women as men, as was the street sale. The egg throw and firemen's water fight were attended mainly by men. Attendance at the street carnival also varied by sex: the "kiddy rides" attracted women with young children, whereas the faster and more dangerous rides attracted late teen-aged women; the bingo stand attracted older women; the electronic game arcade and carnival game booths attracted principally young men, whereas the beer wagon and food stands in the center attracted a great many men and some middle-aged couples. The parade, which attracted many outsiders, was the only event where the sex ratio was approximately equal. The world of men and the world of women, then, do not overlap much more in the festival than they do outside the festival. (Bly [1981] elegantly and sadly discusses this separation). Behavior patterns that characterize everyday life continue during the festival, and indeed are reinforced, since this is the major public event of the Foley secular calendar and the one occasion that serves as a common shared experience.

From this, one may say that the festival serves to intensify and incarnate the innerdirectedness of the community through a dialectic whose terms are participation and self-awareness. The festival is set up in such a way as to minimize participation by non-Foleyites. Thus, although the festival is advertised as beginning on a Saturday, the only events of that day are a mini-marathon and the first day of the Softball Tournament, both of which attract outside participants. Indeed, it is noteworthy that most of the runners in the former event are not from Foley. Relatively few spectators are found at these events, and any would-be spectators are discouraged from attending the race, as it is scheduled in the morning along a route that takes it out of town, rather than into it.

The part of the festival that is most significant to Foleyites begins on Sunday night with the queen pageant, which attracts one-fourth of the town's population. The events following the queen pageant are for internal consumption only, deliberately scheduled during the week, thus limiting attendance to those who are in the immediate area. People who live at any significant distance cannot attend, since they must work during the day or the next morning.

The festival concludes with a large parade that includes many high-school bands, some from as far away as the Twin Cities. People from all over the area flock to the parade, which is the region's largest. One year attendance was estimated at 13,000.

To summarize, Foley Fun Days begins and ends with events which attract outsiders, with the inner core aimed at locals. Hence, the resulting pattern brings local people together and then sets them apart from the outsiders at the parade. This movement through Fun Days thus symbolizes the community's separateness from the surrounding area. At the same time, however, the separateness is also created and reinforced by the movement. Foley Fun Days, like other festivals (cf. Buechler 1980), operates on several levels simultaneously. It is the self-reflexivility implied by this that makes the festival potent.

Waterama

The pattern in Foley contrasts sharply with the situation in Glenwood, where the organization is fundamentally bureaucratic and hierarchical. The Glenwood Waterama is a corporation, associated with the Chamber of Commerce, whose purpose is to produce the festival. In overall control is a triumvirate designed to ensure that an experienced leader will always be present: a man, when he accepts the lowest office (vice-commodore) of the triumvirate, accepts a three-year hitch in which he will rise to commodore the second year and admiral the third. There is a constant infusion of new members into the controlling hierarchy; in the history of Waterama there has never been anyone who has repeated the cycle. Additionally, the festival organization is handled by committees of three couples, each of which is in charge of a single event. Once again, the circulating model characteristic of the triumvirate prevails, although it is not insisted upon. In contrast to the festival leadership, in some cases the same people have been in charge of certain activities more than once, and sometimes for many years.

It is of interest to note that there is an essential equality among the committees at this level, and there is no formal mechanism whereby someone starts in a particular committee and works his way up through increasingly important committees until he/she reaches the triumvirate. Some bounce from committee to committee, others put in three years on one committee and never get involved again, whereas some move rather rapidly into the hierarchy.

Unlike Foley Fun Days, power in the Glenwood Waterama does not reside in one person over time, but rather circulates in this quasi-corporate model. Thus the festival text presents an image of orderliness, efficiency, fairness, receptivity to newcomers and new ideas, and "the American Way." That the committees are made up of couples is also an important

difference between Glenwood and Foley. Although men
formally receive credit on the Waterama letterhead, it is clear
to all participants that the work is done by groups of couples
who see planning for Waterama as an occasion for socializing,
as well as a duty to the festival and the community.

Recruitment to the organizational structure also
underlines a significant difference between the two
communities. In Glenwood, the vice-commodore chooses the
vice-commodore for the next year. It is generally agreed that he
should choose a friend, or someone he knows fairly well, since
for the next two years they will be working together
intensively. In this way, year after year a chain forms,
symbolizing the connection of the essential bonds of a
community like Glenwood: friendship and civic responsibility.
Business or professional success is also emphasized, since
members of the triumvirate must be in the type of position
where they can afford to take considerable time from work.

Recruitment to the committees is also along friendship
lines: couples who know each other tend to volunteer to work on
the same committees. Newcomers to the community, once they
have had a chance to establish themselves in a business or
profession may volunteer for a committee or may be asked to
work on Waterama in general or on a particular committee.
Several informants noted that newcomers are given two or
three years "of grace" and then if they have not volunteered are
asked to work on Waterama. A recently arrived lawyer in town
explained his decision to work on the queen coronation
committee: he had to do something, he noted, and so he chose
the committee that required the least work. Social pressure to
participate is strong, and the story is told of a physician who,
upon moving to Glenwood, refused consistently to participate
and found his patients dwindling to such a degree that he left
town. Although there may have been other reasons for his
departure, informants agreed that participation in the
organization of Waterama for at least a few years is absolutely
necessary if a business or professional person wishes to be
accepted into the community. Reasons for this will be
discussed at greater length below.

A final important difference in the organization of the two
festivals concerns the time dimension of the planning process.
The Foley organizer begins to think about Fun Days in late

January, five months before the festival. After Fun Days she does no more work, aside from noting possible changes, until the following January.

In contrast, the Glenwood Waterama has become a year-round activity. There are reports to the board of directors in September, a fund-raising event on Halloween, meetings during winter, a dinner-dance to begin the formal fund-raising in March, and an ever-increasing number of organizational meetings in the spring and summer before the festival takes place on the last weekend in July. For the triumvirate, attendance is required at other festivals every weekend from late May to September. In an important way, Waterama has become the focus of social life in Glenwood for the business and professional communities. It is not an exaggeration to say that what began as a summer festival has become a way of life.

If Foley Fun Days is "inner-directed" the Glenwood Waterama can be termed "outer-directed." Most of the Waterama events are designed to be of interest to outsiders as well as to Glenwood residents. During the three-day festival, 36 events are scheduled. Of these, only five are considered by informants to be "Glenwood events." These are the Button Dance,[2] held on Friday night of the festival, the Kiddie Parade, the Junior Queen Revue, the swimming races, and the community church service. The Button Dance has been part of Waterama since its inception. Wearing a button entitles a person to reduced admission to the dance. Several informants—among them those who swore that they went to no other Waterama events—stated that virtually everyone in the town, regardless of his or her attitude toward the festival, attended the dance. It is the major social event of the year, and a way to see old friends and acquaintances whom one may not encounter during the rest of the year.

The Kiddie Parade has been a part of Waterama for 25 of its 26 years, and attracts a large crowd of Glenwood residents and a few outsiders. The children, all costumed, follow the regular parade route, and compete for prizes in different categories. The smaller children are accompanied by a parent, inevitably the mother. The event serves as a meditation on the passage of time, since the spectators from Glenwood recognize how much the children have grown since the last parade, and also as a symbol (and channel of communication) of the parents' standing in the community, indicated by the elaborateness and costliness of the child's costume. In the same way, the Junior Queen Revue, which is for girls between the ages of 5 to 8, is of principal interest to the local community, and attracts a large crowd. The swimming races too, because they involve local children, are of interest to the community and not to outsiders. The community church service, once a "Galilean Service" that attracted the curious as well as the faithful, is ecumenical and one of the few morning events on Sunday, the last day of the parade. It attracts about 500 people, mostly from Glenwood. All five events, it may be argued, are texts about time and localness in a way the others are not.

The remaining events are scheduled in such a way that the outer-directedness of the festival becomes clear. Waterama opens with the same event that opens Fun Days, a mini-marathon, and, as in Foley, this race attracts many outsiders. The similarities end there. The Waterama race is sponsored by Pepsi-Cola, the Foley race by the local florist. The Foley race is at 9:00 a.m., the Glenwood race at 5:45 p.m. The Waterama race begins on the southern shore of Lake Minnewaska and ends at the hub of festival activities, the city park on the lake. Thus the last two miles take place through crowds, and the finish line is densely packed with spectators who welcome the runners warmly. Food and other refreshments are available after the race from a line of illuminated concession stands along the lakeshore and from the Jaycees chicken barbecue. Winners in each class receive their prizes in front of a large crowd. Accompanying the awards and the barbecue in the early evening is a band concert, followed by the Button Dance.

The two major days of the festival are scheduled to provide a range of activities for various ages and interests, with Saturday designed to reach a peak in the evening, and Sunday to hold spectators from early afternoon until late evening. Even so, the events on both days, even in the mornings, are of general interest. Both days feature art shows, which attract entrants from around the state. Saturday evening begins with another chicken barbecue, followed by a water thrill show by a professional water-ski club, a lighted pontoon parade featuring thematic floats (the only such parade in the Midwest), and an elaborate fireworks display. One year the pontoon parade concerned the months and the seasons, and the subjects depicted symbolize the image the organizers have of themselves and their audience: January was represented by the Super Bowl; winter by Lena and Ole (folkloric Norwegians), snowmobiling, and ice fishing; summer by water sports; and April and December by religious floats. A street sale, which is so important in Foley is also held in Glenwood, but is not as important. Indeed, the Glenwood merchants hold two street sales, one a week before Waterama, so the community residents can have first choice in the sale merchandise.

The major events on Sunday begin with a parade of more than a hundred units, highlighted by bands, floats, and entertainment from around the state. The parade attracts some 20,000 people, and ends at the city park, bringing with it much of the crowd. That crowd is held there by a band concert, a winner-take-half-the-pot bingo game, food and a repeat of the water-thrill show. The festival ends with the coronation of the new Waterama Queen. This event attracts an enormous crowd because it features a well-known state personality every year as master of ceremonies, and because the queen's first official act is to draw the name of a button-purchaser, who wins $2,000. The coronation, which lasts an hour, is followed by a dance with a well-known band.

In sum, the organization of Waterama is designed to attract outsiders. Participation in the festival, however, provides two levels of text: participation in the organization and staging of the events provides one having to do with community service, friendship and the like; participation in the events themselves provides a common experience not unlike that of Foley Fun Days, but with a different accent. The participant from Glenwood is aware that many of the people around him are strangers who are looking at his community and his festival from an outsider perspective. Participation, therefore, is always tinged with otherness and self-awareness, and the focus of the festivals is on a group membership different from that of Foley. Throughout the festival, the Glenwood resident is aware that most of the people around him are others, looking at his home and his efforts as entertainment, missing the subtle ties of participation, consuming what has been painstakingly put together. The Glenwood resident is always self-aware in a way that the

Foleyite is not, for the common experience of those in Glenwood is that of displaying their community to an outside audience as well as revealing it to themselves.

Conclusion: Two Festivals, Two Texts

To have said all this is hardly to have exhausted the levels of meaning and interpretation in these two festivals, as there are significant differences in social control, in the participation of women, in commercial orientation, and more. It is possible, however, to come to some conclusions, and to reexamine what these two cultural texts are saying about and to the communities out of which they spring, for what they say goes beyond the mere reflection of social structure. By providing a concrete, visible distillation of social structure and of social ideas about structure in which virtually the entire community participates, festivals have a transformative potential as well.

It has already been noted that, in Foley, the festival provides a meta-commentary on traditional sex roles. It also provides a metasocial text on the structure of Foley society and the changes which are already affecting that structure. The traditional elite of Foley, small but powerful, are involved only peripherally in Fun Days; they sell hot dogs and hamburgers for the voluntary organizations to which they belong, help organize the parade, and take their children to the carnival. They are content to allow the organizer, a self-made woman, to continue to create a festival which is a metaphor for the traditional structure of the community and in which everyone—men, women, children, merchants, farmers, laborers and professionals—plays his or her accustomed role. The organizer, herself, it can be argued without violating certain confidences, represents the quintessential image of the "good" working class held by the upper and upper-middle classes, and her position at the head of the festival may be seen perhaps as a reward for a life well lived, as an exemplum for others of her station to follow, and certainly as a reinforcement of the traditional social structure. But, as indicated earlier, Foley is changing—there is some industry in the town now, and more and more residents in the town and the surrounding farm areas hold jobs in St. Cloud. The traditional innerdirectedness of the community is changing, and there are corresponding pressures to change the festival. These pressures center around four people who represent a significant challenge to the traditional order, as they all have an orientation that is directed outside Foley.

These four people—a Minneapolis-raised school teacher married to a Foley resident, a nurse at the St. Cloud hospital, the owner of a bar/dancehall and the scion of the most important family in town—symbolize the changes in Foley. These changes are greater participation in the regional economy and culture, more education (especially for women), and the emergence of a new elite whose fundamental orientation is outside the immediate area. These people, all in their late twenties and thirties, represent a far greater threat to the traditional structure than did the Jaycees when they took over the festival. The latter were too young, too concerned with establishing themselves in business, and perhaps too unsophisticated. There is conflict brewing in Foley over control of the town, and Fun Days will be—indeed, already is—one of the areas in which the conflict will surface. If festivals are texts, they are texts that are constantly being revised, and I believe that within a rather short time, there will be a major revision—a fourth edition, as it were—of Foley Fun Days, one which will both express and clarify a major change in the social fabric.[3]

The situation in Glenwood is quite different. Indeed, it might be argued that Waterama exists in its present form to provide stability in the face of nearly constant change in personnel. In a community with such a high rate of turnover in its commercial and professional establishment, a mechanism is needed to integrate newcomers quickly into the community. In Glenwood, Waterama is that mechanism. It provides a way for newcomers to meet other like-minded residents quickly, to have them make a contribution to the community in a highly visible fashion, and to provide the business and professional communities with cross-cutting ties that are neither kin- nor residence-based. Waterama provides the social and civic continuity that is provided in other communities by the transfer of businesses either to relatives or to other relatively long-term residents of the community. Waterama, in an important sense, *is* Glenwood; not unlike a corporate lineage group, it has been the immutable core in the face of the coming and going of businessmen, bankers, automobile dealers, lawyers, newspaper editors, bakers, teachers, and clergy.

The Glenwood Waterama is a text for a mobile society; by and for the middle class, it expresses civic duty, moderation, order, organization, companionate marriage, family entertainment, competition and a certain kind of anonymity. There is little if anything in Waterama that speaks of Glenwood's historical past or ethnic traditions. The festival is highly enjoyable, extremely well organized and beautifully set. (That an outsider should respond in this way is hardly surprising—much of the text is addressed to us, and it is well written.) The point here is that the festival is not so much about an historical Glenwood as it is about the middle class and its manifestations in Glenwood today. This is perhaps best exemplified by a major change in Waterama: the 1980 city ordinance prohibiting the consumption of alcoholic beverages on public property. By 1979, public drinking, especially in the city-owned campground, had become a major problem to many people involved with Waterama. Although there were no serious incidents, there was concern that it was only a matter of time before something unfortunate occurred.

The argument before the city council was that the reputation of the town and of Waterama would be harmed by the drinking—that families and decent people would no longer attend if the festival became known as a drunken orgy. The counter-argument that a number of people involved in the drinking at the campground were young former residents who came home only for Waterama, and that they never left the campground, was less important than the argument that the drinking represented a threat to the festival. The ordinance passed, the campground was closed, and drinking in public was prohibited. The fear of the opponents of the ordinance— that it would kill the festival—seemed groundless, as subsequent years have been extremely successful. Moderation and family entertainment seem to have won out over licence in a way that Elias (1978) sees as characteristic of the middle class, and which is certainly characteristic of what may be termed the bourgeoisation of traditional carnivals (see, for example, Lavenda 1980, for this process in late nineteenth-century Caracas).

A conclusion can thus be reached regarding the transformative, dialectical nature of festivals. The controversy over drinking in Glenwood is not a straightforward reflection of social structure, nor is it a reflection of regular factions within the society; people who ordinarily agreed on other issues disagreed about the drinking problem and its solution. Rather, it seems to have been part of a series of adjustments, interpretations if you will, concerning the best way to achieve what virtually all agreed was the basic meaning of the festival. Once the adjustments were made, with the text not only reinterpreted but also revised, the new interpretations became potent. That the change had been made at all told people something of importance; that they could live with it and enjoy it told them something of importance too. For the power of a text is precisely that it is said—whether the frame be fiction, play or jest. Having once been said, it is part of our experience, part of the reflective ground of our interpretation of life. Festivals are indeed "for fun," but in having fun we say, and learn, a lot about ourselves.

Notes

Research during 1981 was made possible by a faculty-student research grant from the Bush Foundation. My thanks to Marybeth Christenson-Jones, Gina Dircks, Roger Maltais, and the SCSU Sociology/Anthropology and Social work Department faculty seminar participants' comments on a draft of this paper. Special thanks to Rita Erickson for sharing some of her research findings in Foley with me, and especially to Emily Schultz for a thorough-going, detailed reading of the paper.

[1]The development corporation had hoped to be able to attract a substantial amount of light industry to the area, but by 1981, had succeeded in bringing in only two manufacturing firms. One was forced to close, putting nearly 200 people out of work, and the other had to lay off some 75 people.

[2]The "button" referred to is a circular pin, like a political candidate's button, which is sold for $2.00 in the stores and on the street during Waterama. It is the principal fund-raising source for the festival, and brought in $15,000 in 1981.

[3]After this paper was completed, word was received from Foley that Fun Days would no longer be held. Shortly thereafter, phoenix-like, Fun Days was resurrected by a new group. The old organizer was pointedly not invited to attend the organizational meeting, and the individuals identified above assumed positions of power.

Part III

Sporting Spectacles

Chapter 4

Will the Sheik Use His Blinding Fireball?
The Ideology of Professional Wrestling

Jim Freedman

The advance men for the travelling wrestling show had come to Simcoe, Ontario, a week before the show to do the publicity. They taped show cards wherever shopkeepers would not mind, to gas station walls, to the outside of the abandoned storefront windows. A casual clutch of middle-aged men stood facing one of the signs. COMING SOON, it was headlined. One man, younger and more ragged than the rest, read the sign slowly with his mouth. "The Sheik. More unpopular than ever. Superstar of the mat." He surveyed the three or so photographs. There was one where the Sheik gnashed his teeth against the bloody face of an opponent. In another, a bolt of fiery light flashed from the Sheik's upraised hand. "Will the Sheik use his BLINDING FIREBALL???" read the caption. As a couple of men departed, one and then another approached and read the sign over. A stout man in the rear muttered the whole thing was phoney. He worked his way closer to the sign. "That one there," he said, animated. "I seen that one on TV. He'll get tore up." A moment later, he spotted his wife, returned from shopping at an uptown store. Her upper teeth were missing. "Hey, Midge," he asked, "Wanna see the rassling?"

August is a kind of Christmas in Simcoe. It is the season for making money and for spending it. Simcoe lies in the center of Ontario's tobacco belt, a long stretch of flat land parallel to Lake Erie's northern shore. Tobacco is grown in prudishly straight lines so that the harvesting rigs, mounted by laborers, can make their way down ten rows at a time. Migrant workers flood the tobacco towns in late August. Simcoe's population stands at 14,000 in winter. In summer, swollen by students, Mexicans, Quebecois, and others who come in busloads and caravans of elderly two-barrelled cars, the population rises to almost 20,000.

August is the time when wrestling shows make money in Simcoe. The migrant workers make up a good part of the audience, but the local residents are there too: the farmers, the shift-workers in Simcoe's largest plant, the American Can Company of Canada, the shopkeepers and others. Public life is at its peak. There are barbecues and baseball. Football season has opened in the bars. It is still warm. It is Simcoe's Saturnalia. Wrestling fans who, year-round, watch matches on Saturday afternoon television look forward to this time of the year when, as in the old days, wrestling comes live to the town arena.

Here is professional wrestling in its original form, set amidst the fervent passions of a small town. The streets are narrow, the lives are public. Individuals stand out in this small social world so that stark differences are noticeable between one sort and another, between genuine and confederate sorts, between rich and poor. There is here a whole social world that people can and do take notice of: they take notice of lapses in morality, of who does not attend the church barbecues, of who is good and who is impeccably correct, of the unkempt manners of late August's itinerants.

Thirty years ago professional wrestling thrived in this setting. Well-known wrestlers travelled the circuit in those days, from town to town where they were meaningful heroes. Each town knew them. Towns-folk embraced some and rejected others. The wrestlers were moral and immoral, baby faces or villains, confronting each other in full view where the towns-folk could see the fates of the demi-gods and demons of the ring. And in the fates of these caricatures of good and evil, they saw their own fates, they saw themselves and their neighbors and what they could become in the universe of their town. In the past thirty years, things have changed. Not the town but the wrestling. Wrestling has abandoned the small towns for the international world of television. The money is now made in the big city forums and domes. In these big-town arenas wrestling still plays on small-town sentiments, and as long as such sentiments survive, wrestling will always have a place. But big-town wrestling and its TV stations have taken the boy out of the country. They have wrested it from the moorings. Wrestling's real past, and the mythological present from which it will ever draw its meaning, is in small towns like Simcoe.

The night of the wrestling a crowd came early. A line started at the door and went around the side and toward the back of the building where the back doors of the American Can Company of Canada plant faced onto the street. The night shift worked inside. Day-shift workers stood among the fans in line and shouted at the night crew. The arena doors opened at 8:00 p.m. Louis Ariba Martinez came up from the dressing room to sign souvenir photos at the picture table. One of the midgets on the card came to help with the tickets.

Billy the Red Lion from Hamilton, in red trunks, opposed Al Costello from Australia, wearing an outback jacket, boomerang, and green trunks. The fans cheered Billy the Red, a local favorite. First Costello tortured Billy. There were groans and pain sounds from clean-looking Billy as Costello, the man of a thousand holds, held the upper hand. Then Costello whipped Billy the Red against the ropes and met him on the rebound with an abdominal thrust. Costello had something hidden in his pants, a pencil maybe; this was dirty fighting. The crowd screamed revenge. Costello is not above pulling some dirty stuff, said a grey-haired woman next to me. Costello started jabbing with the object in his pants and the lady got out of her seat to scream at the referee. The referee looked but failed to call a foul. Then Billy decided to give Costello some of his own medicine. Billy seized the sharp object and jabbed away at Costello. No one breathed a word to the referee. Billy took Costello's two legs, spread them wide apart in front of him and checked himself as he prepared to kick Costello in the groin. Billy yelled to the audience: *Should I?* and they said *Yeah*. Again he asked and again they said *Yeah*. And he delivered a mighty blow that sent Costello writhing out of the ring. Billy pulled him back, put one foot on either side of the corner post so that Costello was straddling the post and half hanging out of the ring. Billy yelled to the crowd, *Should I Pull?* The answer was *Yeah!* And he jammed Costello's groin against the post. Billy was on the way to victory, but Costello had hidden his sharp thing in Billy's pants and, shortly after, by the referee's decision, Billy was disqualified. Billy flew into a rage. The crowd was furious.

Liberal Ideology in the Ring

For the French scientist of signs, Roland Barthes, wrestling is rich territory. In one very important sense, these characters are on parade more than in combat: who they are is more important than either how they play or whether they win or lose. Fighters come out defining themselves more than fighting. When Billy the Red fought the Sheik in Simcoe two weeks later, the Sheik emerged in a $500 suit and then changed into his wrestling costume, highlighted by one dangerously pointed shoe, and a yellow chiffon cape, which Billy quickly wrapped around the Sheik's head as the crowd shrieked in delight. Billy, on the other hand, like other clean fighters, dresses without shoes, belts, capes and hats—without such adulterations to the human wrestling body. Some fighters stereotype themselves as evil and some do not.

Barthes (1972) contrasts wrestling with boxing. Boxing is a model form of pure competition. Fight-fixing aside, the fighters come together as two opposed forces, to be resolved by a test of skill into one winner in the course of the fight. Nothing is given in advance of the fight to predict or prejudice the outcome. This is what makes gambling on the outcome so intense. Professional wrestling, however, begins with a message: that there are good guys and bad guys, and that the objective of the match is not to resolve good and bad but simply to define and dramatize this opposition. If boxing seeks a resolution in one victor, wrestling seeks not to come to a resolution through victory, but in format of combat to elaborate conflict.

But there is more. It is a fact that matches do not pit individuals as much as the idea of good versus bad in the ring. Nevertheless it is important to note that the fight goes on as if it were a regular competition, with referees (the referee even carries a sign, to wit: OFFICIAL REFEREE) and rules, to designate a winner, who is, only too often, the bad guy. This takes the message of the match one step further. In Barthes'

(1972) description, the French wrestling form delights mainly in discovering the essence of the officially repugnant character, the *salaud* or the bastard. The Simcoe matches teach another, grander and more repulsive lesson: that liberal ideology is bankrupt, not because it is inherently untrue and inappropriate—liberal ideology is, after all, all that the members of the audience, for the most part, have and believe in. It does not work because it is foiled by evil forces. By adulterated human forces. That is why nice guys finish last.

When the bad guy wins, liberal ideology loses. This is obvious from how the good guys stereotype themselves. And when it happens it is very interesting. In London, Ontario, following the disqualification of the noble peasant Mighty Igor, in a match with the evil Sheik, children screamed and women cried in anger. An old man, barely able to walk, hobbled to the stage and flailed wildly at the escaping Sheik with his cane. People become very angry when the bad guy wins, because justice is being taken for a ride.

This behavior says a lot about the spectators. It implies, and quite correctly, that for many of them moral indignation is a frequent state of mind. Who are these spectators? First of all, as we have said, they are citizens of small towns. Behavior, being more public, brings the issues of good and bad, of chivalry and villainy more commonly into scrutiny. Wrestling in a town such as Simcoe provides a spectacle about one of the major issues of small-town life: right and wrong conduct.

More recently, though, the composition of the viewers has changed from that of the rural villagers to urban labor. These are low-income workers, immigrants, welfare recipients, those for whom the gates of success are closed in what they have heard is the land of free opportunity. For them the forces of evil, the forces which subvert the ideals of the liberal society, loom uncommonly large. One finds that the majority of the spectators, though by no means all, are the disenfranchised, and wrestling is their story. For them, the paradoxical role of evil, of the villain, is what they come to observe. Cheating and dirty work in the ring, like cheating in the marketplace, is counter to all their ideals, yet it provides paradoxically the only exit from their own poverty. Wrestling says to them that they have two choices: one is to work honestly forever and never make it; the other is to take shortcuts and succeed from down

Good and evil compete for public attention on a wrestling card

under by signing on with the devil. Wrestling is the story of the disenfranchised; good, honest men meeting misfortune in the land of equality. This is the message which wrestling brings to its urban audience. In this sense, wrestling is, as Manning has characterized celebration in the introduction to this volume, "an artifact which informs its social context." Through wrestling, the viewers come to understand and thereby express the failure of their expectations.

This said, wrestling strikingly resembles another public spectacle artfully described by Geertz (1972): the cockfight in Bali. The cockfights no more involve cocks than the wrestling involves men. At stake in the cockfight are the cocks' owners; as Geertz says, it is men and not cocks fighting. Just so, it is not individual men, but types of men at stake in the wrestling ring. Such gala plays seem to appeal to the margins of society where discontent is festering and where matters of substantial complexity, such as social stratification, social mobility or its absence, can be given simple handles. The cockfights are illicit performances and take place in the shadows; wrestling, while not illicit, is strictly supervised by public officials, and has a reputation as a "low-class," inferior form of entertainment.

In Bali, it is said that the people are greatly concerned about their public appearances, public and social roles, and about saving face. Shame they fear most of all. When a cock fights, in some important measure so do its owners. When a cock wins, the winner prunes his feathers and collects his bets. But when a man's cock loses, he has lost not only his bets, his cock, but, his manhood, his face. He has died a social death. The dramatic metaphor is about the stakes involved in intense public interaction. It draws less directly from the politics of the society than wrestling, but like wrestling, it is a public spectacle of misfortune, of the misery of shame. When the good guy loses in wrestling, there is likewise a sense of terrible misfortune. Justice is caricatured as an evil and harsh instrument. These plain and brutal messages, Geertz says, in general are "unprogressive and generally unbecoming an ambitious nation" (1972:2).

Love and Money

Since professional wrestling largely defines and

dramatizes forces of good and evil, it is no surprise that much of what goes on involves articulating wrestling lore, creating stereotypes.

The wrestlers do it when they seize the mike before and after matches, when they dress, and in the course of interviews in the many "official" wrestling magazines. Representations of wrestlers arrange them neatly into good and bad. Don "Bull Dog" Kent wears a dog collar around his neck and has few friends. He says: "I don't have any friends in professional wrestling for the simple reason I don't want or need them. People try to be my friends, but that is only because they are hoping some of my stardom will rub off on them. My only friend is DOLLARS." Hank James says much the same and has come to be known as Hank "Money Man" James. Few of the unpopular wrestlers enter the ring because they love the sport or because they love the fans, or for the thrill of competiton. They fight for dollars, to win, and in the case of the most despicable, such as the Sheik, they may even fight for the love of violence.

The popular wrestlers love the sport and the fans. Handsome Ramon Rougeau is a favorite with the ladies. He is in it because his father was a great wrestler, and he wants to emulate him. He is not unlike the Fabulous Funk Brothers, Terry and Dory, sons of Dory Senior; these siblings aim to uphold the name of their father. It is said of Dory Junior that he is a smooth grappler and rarely explodes. He prefers a good wrestling hold to anything, but he is not afraid to pull some illegal moves if he has to. The popular wrestlers stress that they are fighting *for someone*, sometimes for a blood relative, often for the fans whom they seek to please by their skill. The unpopular ones, such as Tony Marino, may say: "Who needs friends—all I want is victories." They work to win, and also inevitably for "money." Blood is opposed to money, relationship opposed to ego. Kin obligations are more important than seeking personal gain; people are more important than things.

How they wrestle is even more informative. Some of the standard dramatic conventions of the event itself, the theatrical techniques of the wrestlers, have been artfully described some years ago (Craven and Mosely 1972). The most important of these conventions are those that distinguish the baby-face from the villain, since these serve to link the one and the other to models of real public citizens. The good guys are recognized as skillful wrestlers who rely on their training, their hard work, their unadulterated human talent. It is individual strength and will which take them onto the mat. Others, the villains, attempt to bring in something more than their natural human endowment: Eric the Red carries an enormous bone into the ring. Stan "the man" Stasiak holds in reserve the heart punch, an illegal but deadly move. Victor Rivera has aligned himself with a manager who accompanies him to fights holding a putter, and other wrestlers bring buddies along to help them out of tight spots. The Kangaroo tag team claim to have *science* on their side; it is their secret scientific approach which makes the Canadian wrestlers afraid of them. As for the Sheik, we can only speculate whether it is his manager, Eddie the "Brain," who gives him his uncanny ability to win. We know that the Sheik carries around a pet snake and a small metal awl in his pointed shoe. But it is his mind which poses the greatest mystery of all, for as the publicity posters remind us: "Who knows what evil lurks in the mind of the Sheik?" The Sheik will not say, for he does not talk.

An evening's wrestling inclines a viewer to choose between two different perspectives on the daily struggle to get ahead within the Canadian or American political economy. If the good guy wins, then it seems the more likely that there is equal opportunity for everyone; that everyone is given more or less the same endowments, and that by virtue of our liberal democracy, we all have the same rights and privileges. If we use our unadulterated human endowment with strength, training and goodwill, then our reward is forthcoming. It is not for nothing that we argue for liberty and private enterprise, for these are cornerstones of the theory: that each individual, alone, is and should be responsible for whatever destiny befalls. This destiny is impeded by neither greed, nor nepotism nor prejudice nor, even technology. Theoretically, any fighter, if he trains and is skillful, can win by his natural endowments. But if the bad guy wins, this makes credible a very different interpretation of politics and economy. It says that devices, deceit and technology make a sham of the fact that people come to society with equal opportunity. It does not deny that people begin with equal endowments or that society should provide, accordingly, equal opportunity. These are righteous truths. It simply says that without some adulteration of natural endowments, without something apart from natural human skill, the individual fighter seldom has a chance. This may be the bone of Eric the Red, or the evil that lurks in the mind of the Sheik. Almost all wrestling events bear out this latter interpretation,. Well over half of the matches are won by bad guys. For southwestern Ontarians this means that in spite of their good intentions and the widely recognized civility of which they are proud, as laborers and farmers they get little for being nice guys. The spoils go to those who use shortcuts or tricks, who play on others' fears, who care only about money and not people, who are profligates, fags, Arabs, Greeks, Germans, Americans, Australians, imponderably obese and given to violence. Just as blue and white collars confront each other, so do fighters. The white collars have extra endowments: they are technically assisted, they turn politics to advantage, they wear sun glasses; they use putters; they are adulterated in some form or other.

There is a moral and political battle going on. Not between two individuals but between two explanations of how individuals fare in their daily affairs; one is the *ideology* of capitalism—that is, that all men are equal in the market place—the other, the *practice* of capitalism—that is, that good, honest men are at a distinct disadvantage. They are significantly very different. The ideology of capitalism, that is democratic liberalism, is attested to only by exceptions which miraculously prove the rule, exceptions such as the odd, decent fighter Dominic Denucci, who wins. Greed, the practice of capitalism, is what really prevails over human behavior. It is a painful lesson, dark and truthful: that nice guys really finish last, that the ideology of contemporary western society is a failure.

The lesson is all the more dramatic and credible because it is put to the test in that most exemplary of all trials: the boxing ring, with a referee and rules. An announcer gives the fighters' weights. It is important not to forget that even though the characters are elaborately stereotyped, the audience still perceives them as fighting, as working out their differences according to the rules of the ring. This is why, when evil vanquishes, the loss of liberalism is so very decisive.

Understanding this form, the ring, in which the encounter of the ideology and the practice of capitalism fight it out, is absolutely crucial to understanding the meaning of the event. No one perceives the fight as a morality play. What arouses us is that the ring is, after all, one of North America's select arenas for perfect competition. A recent match between the hated Sheik and a well-liked opponent made this very clear. The match was declared invalid because the Sheik left the ring and ran from the scene. The opponent seized a loose two-by-four stud and chased the Sheik from the auditorium. The crowd was enraged with the decision to invalidate the match, and shortly after an unidentified representative from the Ontario wrestling council made a noteworthy decision. The Sheik was to return to the ring with his opponent in two weeks' time, but this time the ring would be replaced by a locked steel cage where the fighters would meet in combat without—and here is an important fact—without the referee. This, he declared, would be a fair match. One man would leave the cage victorious.

The renowned credibility of the ring can have a number of different impacts on the viewers. For viewers prone to be skeptical, the total event seems even less credible, simply because by all appearances, the best fighter should at least sometimes win. This of course need never happen because it is not the meaning of the matches. But for such viewers the contradiction between appearances—that is, the ring—and the fact of imperfect competition or no competition at all, is too much to swallow. It is a contradiction between the form and the substance of the event, one so great that it discredits the entire activity.

For others, such a contradiction is no problem. For the real fans of wrestling a contradiction between the ideas, the ideology, or the ideal format for how individuals succeed, and the fact of just how many people actually do succeed within and according to this format, is quite understandable. It is perhaps the most important thing that they know. A lot of them vote for the more conservative party in order to rectify this situation and to force certain persons to adhere to the format more closely than they do.

Few, however, no matter how they vote, have any real illusions about where government stands. Putting one's hope in government is like putting one's hope in the referee, and this is obviously silly. The referee is a perpetual source of disappointment. While properly attired, he never successfully administers the rules. He consistently fails to see the illegal holds or catch sight of the small devices the dirty wrestlers use in the ring. He may even inadvertently miss a legitimate victory by a decent wrestler. This does not render the referee superfluous, as some skeptics might suspect, but makes him the key to an arousing performance. Here is evoked the analogy between the fight and the daily struggles of people who rely on rules to protect them against abuses of the system. The referee is, if not explicitly, at least implicitly, the government whose ineffectualness leads inevitably to the failure of the ideology it so righteously espouses. His failure excuses the rules and condemns their application. He makes the blatant unrestrained excesses of the bad guys all the more repugnant and credible.

Finally, the failure of the referee leaves a gap where authority ought to be. It begs to be filled, and the audience, right on cue, respond as vigilantes. Kids throw paper cups at the bad guy; women and men rush to the ringside to warn a good guy of an illegal device the dirty wrestler has hidden in his shoe. It may lead, for example, to a man's picking up his folding chair and, as I witnessed in surprise, flinging it toward the dirty wrestler shouting, "Asshole of the Universe." His wife, her fists clenched in rage, wondered aloud how the referee could be so stupid. It is better than voting. In the territorial melee I, too, was screaming abuses at the referee. Something was terribly wrong and we were going to make it right.

One of the fascinating facts of wrestling is its perception by the skeptics, a great majority of our friends and neighbors. Thinking about this perception may lead us to a fundamental lesson about the persistence of a prevailing, dominant ideology. For the skeptics, the fundamental truths of existence are being challenged in the wrestling ring. These truths are that pure competition does exist and that anything which asserts the contrary is invalid. Or worse, it is a deception, a fake. What is wrong with wrestling, they say, is that it does not properly depict real life; it is, quite simply, wrong. The dominant ideology responds to the challenge which wrestling poses to its practice quite simply by declaring that such fighting, such an event, is false.

Of course, the fights are rigged, just as theatre is rigged. But like theatre, it is hard to keep this in mind at ringside. One elderly gentleman reckoned that "a lot of it may be false, sure, but at some point it gets pretty hot and heavy and he sure as hell wouldn't want to be in there."

Some blows may purposefully miss their mark, but most fans deny this is true for all of them, and the fighters insist that it is never true. What is going on is that a good guy is trying to make the world safe for liberal democracy and he is losing. And he is getting no help from the people who say this is how things ought to be and who are supposed to enforce the rules. And if they are of no help then the people must take matters into their own hands. By this time, the fight is in the streets.

After the match, the Simcoe arena opened onto a small street across from a park. On the way home a number of young boys who had been inside started a scuffle and soon there was a brawl. Somebody pulled a knife.

Chapter 5

Get Some Money for Your Honey: Gambling on the Wages of Sin

Frank E. Manning

"Get some money for your honey.... Come in here on a bike, go home in a Rolls Royce.... Take your hands out of your pocket and put your money on the table.... Wall Street slumps, but this stock market pays double...."

This is the language of the "stock market," a gambling tent found at cricket festivals in Bermuda. In it are about forty tables for crown and anchor, a fast-paced dice game that attracts a holiday crowd ranging from onlookers and casual bettors to high-stakes gamblers. In a day, a half-million dollars changes hands.

This scenario is a cultural variant on North American casino gambling and captures two of its essential features: (1) the rapid acquisition and expenditure of money; and (2) the heady ambience and social style of the environment, which gamblers themselves diffusely describe as "the action." As Goffman (1961), Wolfe, (1966) and other popular ethnographers of the Las Vegas scene remind us, these two features combine to give the casinos their powerful appeal. Gambling, then, is both money and symbolism, bread and circuses. Gain and loss are experientially inseparable from the participatory performance of betting.

Recent studies of gambling have keyed on some correspondences with other social and cultural forms. Geertz' (1972) analysis of betting at the Balinese cockfight is a case in

80

point. Regarding casino gambling in the United States, Abt and Smith (1983) argue that it does not challenge cultural values, although it may appear that way: rather, like other forms of popular entertainment, gambling reflects and reaffirms the central tenets of the culture. It is an example of "money buying experience," and thus an apotheosis of consumer capitalism and the modern American dream. Their views are drawn, in part, from those of Herman, who laments the tendency of researchers to approach gambling as psychological or criminal deviance. "What we need," he contends, "is more work designed to place gambling in context ... looking at it not as an aberration of central themes and values in culture, but as an understandable expression of those themes and values..." (1976: xi).

Yet the simple fact that gambling has often been studied as deviance should not be overlooked, for this perspective also reflects important cultural values. In North America's dominant Protestant cultures, gambling has traditionally been stigmatized as sinful and socially corrupting. Even today, while gambling spreads rapidly in some parts of the United States, it remains taboo in the Bible Belt and other conservative areas.

The controversy over gambling is telescoped in Bermuda, a circum-Caribbean island inundated by American influences of both secular and religious varieties. Gambling epitomizes one set of Bermudian cultural values, and flaunts another. The conflict, which is "played out" in the stock market, also has striking political significance. The stock market scenario is a rendition of, and commentary upon, the structure of Bermudian power relations.

Betting in Style

Summer in Bermuda is enlivened by a variety of festivals which, like virtually all other facets of social life, correspond closely to the fundamental and intractable division between whites, about two-fifths of the population, and blacks, the remainder. White festivities are marked by sailing competitions, notably the renowned Newport-Bermuda race. These events are "highlights of the social season," opportunities for upper-class and upwardly mobile whites to ritualize status affinities with the international yachting elite, and, not incidentally, to strike marital alliances and business compacts.

Black celebrations revolve around cricket, a sport introduced by the British but gradually taken over by blacks and, as in the Caribbean generally, transformed into an important symbol and vehicle of black advancement (James 1963; Manning 1973). Bermuda's oldest cricket festival, Cup Match, is a two-day event commemorating emancipation from slavery. Played between clubs at opposite ends of the island, it is roughly, in its festive extravagance, a Bermudian equivalent of carnival celebrations in the eastern Caribbean. There are also three series of "county games," each consisting of a play-off tournament between workmen's clubs that have long-standing, colorful rivalries.[1]

Unlike regular league games which draw mainly from cricket *afficionados,* the festivals attract mass crowds whose attention is generally less occupied by the contest on the field than by the pleasures of indulgent drinking, the gustatory delights of traditional "soul" foods (notably cassava pie, conch stew, shark hash, mussel pie, and richly cooked meats piled on black-eye peas and rice), the patterned interaction of joking, insult-swapping, and gregarious hospitality, the verbal and kinetic play of initiating or enhancing sexual partnerships, the histrionic display of current Afro-American and Afro— Caribbean fashions, the seductive rhythms of steel bands and Gombey[2] troupes performing on the sidelines, and, in areas staked out by Rastafarian *ganja* smokers, the hypnotic beat of taped reggae music amplified through auditorium-sized electronic speakers. The game is over at dusk, but celebrants remain at the field, sometimes throughout the night, unless they choose to attend one of the dances or shows held in various clubs. As one reveler aptly summarized it, cricket festivals are the time "when we eat everything in Bermuda, drink everything in Bermuda, wear everything in Bermuda, and spend everything in Bermuda."

Along the sidelines of the cricket field stands the stock market, a wood or tubular steel-framed structure covered with canvas or thatch. In it, at the crown and anchor tables, players bet spiritedly on one or more of six items: a red crown, a black anchor, and the four suits of cards. A croupier shakes three

A stock market table operator

dice, their sides corresponding to the betting choices on the table. Winners are paid the amount of their bet times the number of dice on which it is shown, while losers have their money taken by the table. If a croupier rolls a diamond and two anchors, for example, he pays those who bet on the diamond, pays double those who bet on the anchor, and takes the money bet on the other four items.

Each betting round takes less than a minute, giving the game a brisk tempo that contrasts strikingly with the slowness of the cricket match but one that is compatible with the festival ambience. Some players remain at a favorite table for hours, or until their cash and credit are exhausted. Others bet a few times and move on, either to other tables or to festive pursuits outside the stock market.

Crown and anchor is popular among West Indians, particularly at festivals. I have personally watched it played at the Antigua Carnival, on Maroon holidays in Jamaica, and in European gambling houses patronized by Caribbean emigres. In Bermuda, which boasts one of the world's highest per capita incomes, the game is distinguished by its high stakes. The minimum bet is one dollar,[3] but it is only novices and casual players, mostly women, who bet such a small amount. Regular players bet between $10 and $50 each time, although larger bets are common. Some tables have a ceiling on bets, but it is never lower than $100. Tables with large cash floats generally allow unlimited betting.

One might compare the stock market to metropolitan casinos, where the high visibility of money is seen as a major attraction. As Newman observes:

> Men don't come to Las Vegas primarily to look at girls. They come to look at money. Nowhere else . . . is there such an obsession with the actual physical presence of money. There may be other places that induce an awareness of money, where the routinized trappings are such that you realize that money is behind them, but in Las Vegas the money is right out in front. You see it all the time. . . . people walk around with fistfulls of bills, and they are always handling them: playing with them, counting them, rearranging them in neat stacks, passing them back and forth to other people. . . (1962:83-84).

The stock market goes even a step beyond the Las Vegas

casinos. It is actual cash that is bet at the crown and anchor tables, not chips or markers. Croupiers hold thousands of dollars in their hands, flamboyantly displaying them to attract bettors, who are likely to hold several hundred. Commenting on the difference between festival cricket and the Christmas season, an informant observed that at Christmas money is spent, whereas at festival cricket it is both spent and shown.

Like all pivotal symbols, money is ambiguous. It intensifies the risk, excitement, and absorptive grip of the gambling "play world," as Goffman (1961) has labelled it, but it is also the currency of ordinary economic discourse. Other symbols extend this duality of meaning, notably the term "stock market."

As an arena of play, the stock market illustrates Caillois' (1979) four modes of ludic expression and experience: *agon* or competition; *alea* or chance; *ilinx,* literally dizziness or vertigo but more generally what Durkheim (1915) called effervescence; and *mimicry*, deliberate role-taking and performance. This framework has been applied by Herman (1976) to casino and race-track gambling in the United States, principally to establish a typology. I will use it in the same way that Turner also uses it in this volume—to suggest the dynamism and symbolic richness of a playful occasion. As a game crown and anchor may be utterly simple, but as a performance in the stock market, it is semantically complex.

Regular players view stock-market gambling as an intense, personalized competition between themselves and the table operators. The players' aim is not simply to win bets, but to score a decisive victory by "breaking the board." Table operators share this view, although their attention is diffused among several opponents. As one operator put it, "They [players] see your money, and they want to take it all. So you try to take theirs instead."

Occasionally, bettors realize their goal. I am told that one high roller, known appropriately as "Caesar," once broke three boards at a county game, walking away with $44,000. More often, of course, the odds favoring the table prevail. One bettor confessed to having dropped $13,000 in a single afternoon, an episode that, like Caesar's big win, has been immortalized in gambling lore.

Heroic attempts at breaking the board are common when a player has lost substantially, borrowed money to stay in the game, and then started winning to go ahead. Rather than quit, the player succumbs to "greed," with generally predictable consequences. A table operator recalled an occasion when he took all of a player's money, and then lent him $5 for his cabfare home. The player instead took the $5 to another table, and had a winning streak that brought him $1,500. With his appetite whetted, he increased his betting. Eventually he lost both the $1,500 and another $800 that he had borrowed from the second table.

I have observed similar episodes, as this case from my field notes illustrates:

> Placing $10 and $20 bets haphazardly, a man lost his own money—about $60—as well as $50 that he had borrowed from the table. He then borrowed another $50, and increased it to about $85 by winning a few small bets. He next bet $70 on the club, which came up on three dice to add $210 to his money. But although he owed the table $100 he kept playing rather than pay back the debt and quit with a net winning. Within a half-hour he lost all his money, as well as a third loan of $50.

The recklessness of betting lays bare the element of chance, Caillois' second mode of ludic experience. Regular bettors know the arithmetic of probability, and typically advocate "percentage playing" when they discuss the game. At the table, however, their betting tends to be either highly erratic or stubbornly unvaried, as it is dictated by hunches, favorites and bewildering permutations of serendipitous factors. The epitome of this outlook is seen when players stand several feet away from the table, roll up a high denomination bill, and simply throw it on the table, letting chance decide the bet.

Table operators employ their own forms of magic, in the classic Frazerian sense. They invariably carry two sets of dice, and surreptitiously substitute one for the other if they are sustaining heavy losses. Alternately, if a table operator is losing repeatedly, he will pass the dice cup to another croupier, offering the excuse that he has to relieve himself—a break that is seen as ending a run of bad luck. At an extreme, these rituals border on what Levy-Bruhl (1922) termed "mystical thought." A few croupiers, for instance, claim that their powers of concentration are strong enough to control the dice. Rather than shaking the dice and concealing them under the cup while bets are placed, they wait until the money is down, and then, while shaking, exert the appropriate mental influence.

The stock market also has aspects of the type of effervescence and sensory exhilaration that Caillois classified as *ilinx*. The game has a fast, rhythmic, repetitive pace that, like a road march calypso played over and over again at carnival or like a hymn verse sung repeatedly at revival meetings, has an intoxicating effect that intensifies one's involvement in the present surroundings and diminishes other realities. Combined with the effects of liquor and *ganja*, and contextualized within the heady ambience of the festival, this influence makes the stock market a deceptively powerful seduction. Players are said to "lose their head" in the game, a vernacular explanation of what Geertz (1972) terms "deep play." Gamblers cite this tendency as the reason why players abandon rational strategies and do not know when to quit.

Nor are table operators immune from the seduction of high-stakes gambling, particularly when they have undergone the bettor's rollercoaster experience of winning and losing. Beaten badly near the end of the day, an operator was left with only $500 of his original cash float. In "desperation," he instructed one of his croupiers to bet the entire amount at another table. The bet won, as did a second bet of the same amount, financing a drunken celebration that night in a plush restaurant. But what is of interest is that the croupier labelled crown and anchor a "sucker's game," adding, "If I wasn't running a game, I wouldn't go near the stock market."

Finally and perhaps most significantly, the stock market exemplifies deliberate performance, the mode of play that Caillois called *mimicry*. In Caribbean societies, the histrionic acquisition, display and disposal of money are important aspects of what Wilson (1973) terms "reputation," a black-oriented expressive style emphasizing verbal fluency, sexual prowess and potency, "prettiness" (flashy clothes, dazzling jewelry, fashionable grooming, etc.) and "badness" (toughness, swagger, hedonism). Amplifying the warp and woof of the festival as a whole, the stock market is an arena

Promising riches and entertainment, a table operator calls for bets

where reputations are made, flaunted, tested, renewed and, not infrequently, damaged or lost.

Men dress informally in black-American and West Indian clothing styles, often highlighted by a half-dozen gold necklaces and by athletic or tee shirts bearing double-entendres for genitalia and copulation in conjunction with comical inscriptions of invitation, challenge, or *braggadocio*. Croupiers have an advantage over players, as they are better able to enhance clothing fashions with other performative devices—standing on platforms to increase their visibility, flamboyantly barking the familiar calls that promise quick riches, throwing their dice cups high in the air, and demonstrating their spendthrift hospitality by promiscuously handing out one-dollar bills, gregariously offering beers and liquor, even wantonly throwing players' half-empty drinks on the ground and replacing them with a fresh refill.

Croupiers exploit the stock market's sexual license by giving gambling money to girlfriends, and occasionally imported prostitutes, who in return agree to appear in plunging necklines, loosely crocheted blouses, diaphanous tee shirts, abbreviated halter tops, tight shorts, and similar fashions aimed at attracting—and distracting— male gamblers. As a sequel, a few table operators have begun hiring female croupiers.

There are also a growing number of women who are regular players. Most bet in the $1 to $5 category, making their wins and losses less spectacular than those of men, but allowing them to play for longer periods. A few women, however, could be classed as high rollers, notably a stylish, middle-aged tavern owner, who rarely puts less then $50 on the table, typically divided between two or three items.

Male-female interaction at the tables is highlighted by "rapping," a performative verbal exchange that Kochman, taking a male viewpoint, describes as a "colorful way of asking for some pussy" (1970: 146). Consider the following:

> A middle-aged woman was about to bet on a heart, but withdrew the money. The operator countered: "Don't blame me if three hearts come up, lady. 'Cause you and I— I've been looking at you for a long time—I figure our hearts could get together. We don't need no crown and anchor, honey. Our hearts could really do something."

A woman was betting, and winning, on the black choices (spades, clubs, the anchor), which are all at the bottom of the board. The operator tried to persuade her to diversify her betting: "You gotta go topside. No woman in the world is satisfied on the bottom side."

A woman in her early 30s had been breaking even on small bets and drinking heavily. Toward the end of the day she put a double-entendre to the operator: "All I want is a piece of you." He took up the challenge and carried on a series of lewd but playful insults that drew raucous laughter from those at the table. But she got the last word: "Knobby, you wouldn't know what to do if you tripped and fell on top of me."

The stock market, in short, is a rich and varied play world. The gambler "steps out," as Huizinga (1955) would have it, from the realm of ordinary experience into a realm of deliberate pretense and festive fun. But the play world of crown and anchor gambling is significantly related to other realities and modes of thought. It portrays what Cohen (1974) terms "power relations," the social ordering of political and economic processes. Moreover, it situates that portrayal in a context that is ultimately religious and moral.

Money is Green

A striking ethnographic anomaly is seen in the stock market. About a half-dozen tables are run by Azorean Portuguese, Bermuda's entrepreneurial minority. In radical contrast to the black style, the Portuguese operators play quietly and dress plainly, typically in undistinguished trousers and white or solid-colored long-sleeved shirts, open at the collar. They socialize relatively little with bettors, and abstain entirely from festivities peripheral to gambling. They subscribe to some of the same rituals used by the black operators, notably replacing a "cold" set of dice with a substitute or passing the dice cup to an assistant croupier to stop a losing streak. But they also employ technical means of protection, such as having smaller tables, which are easier to keep under surveillance, and putting a wooden border around the tables, which makes it difficult for players to "fly a bet,"

As bets are placed, a Portugeuese table operator checks his money

that is, put money on the table after the dice cup has been raised. Yet despite these inhibitions, the Portuguese tables are always busy, and most of the business comes from blacks. High-stakes players are particularly attracted, as the Portuguese operators are known for carrying large cash floats and having no ceiling on bets.

The Portuguese presence in the stock market is the residue of what was formerly a much higher profile. Credit for introducing crown and anchor to festival cricket is claimed by Manuel de Souza,[4] the son of an Azorean-born farm laborer. Watching the game played in the segregated white section of the race track in the 1930s, de Souza surmised its appeal to blacks and started going to festival cricket matches with a dice cup, a small table, and a tarpaulin that he stretched between trees to make the first crude version of the stock market. His prediction of the game's popularity proved correct, encouraging him to finance more tables in partnership with other Portuguese. The profits launched him on a business path that led to the acquisition of a restaurant, several small farms, and a fleet of taxicabs. "You can say that I owe what I have to crown and anchor," he once told me. "It gave me my start in life."

In the 1960s the black clubs successfully pressed the claim that the stock market should be under their jurisdiction but, in typical fashion, saw themselves as incapable of running it. Alternately, they made the stock market a concession and sold it to de Souza, an arrangement that gave them a cash flow to stock their bars for festivals and that gave de Souza complete control over the gambling operation. He and his partners ran six tables, and he sold the remainder of the space, chiefly to a growing group of Portuguese known for running gambling parties in private homes. His net profits from the stock market during the 1960s, he reports, averaged $30,000 a season.

De Souza secured his position through patronage, the traditional basis of white-black relations. He became a supporter of club building projects, hired black assistants at his tables, and took on as his chief lieutenant a black with a Portuguese surname. Still, by the late 1960s the spectacle of Portuguese winning money from blacks at a black festival had become irreconcilable with the climate fostered by an increasingly vocal black drive for majority rule and nationalism. Black gamblers pressed for more influence in the stock market, and the clubs hesitantly responded. In some cases they sold the concession to a group of black businessmen, and in others they ran the stock market as a club project. A few clubs, however, continued to favor de Souza, and even in the 1980s he has held the concession at some county games.

Along with these changes a growing number of blacks began operating tables, giving the stock market its present, heavily black appearance. As all gamblers know, however, it is just that—an appearance. The black operators, with few exceptions, are unable to bankroll their own tables. Their financial backing comes from unseen "partners," who in most cases are whites or racially mixed syndicates. In return for providing the cash float—as much as $15,000 at some tables— the backers take a 40 percent to 60 percent share of the winnings. The arrangement evokes a strong comparison between the stock market and the wider society: blacks are in visible positions and appear to be making money, but whites are behind them and in control. As one black gambler commented, "You know, come to think of it, I don't know a single black person in this country who has made money without having a white sponsor."

Biracial gambling partnerships active in the stock market also run invitational crown and anchor parties, usually in private homes or rented cottages. One of these normally secretive gatherings was brought to light when a black player lost $27,000 in an all-night game. The money was borrowed in $500 installments from those running the table, a syndicate of two blacks and two whites. When the loser reneged on his debt he was taken to court by the syndicate, but the judge ruled that money loaned specifically for gambling is not retrievable. This benchmark decision does not appear to have curtailed the widespread practice of loaning money at tables, although it has strengthened the resolve of gambling creditors to use more forceful means to collect their debts. Meanwhile, the private games continue, reportedly at stakes that have included real estate properties worth over six figures.

A Bermudian proverb is fittingly introduced here. "Black is black and white is white, but money is green." Culturally different and socially divided, the races are drawn together by the lure of money. But money, to cite another Bermudian proverb, is the "Bermuda Disease." Bermudians, especially blacks, view greed and materialism as major evils in their society. The stock market resonates with both proverbs. It explicitly dramatizes the social evidence that sustains them, and it implicitly enacts and interprets their social consequences.

Metapolitical Commentary

The argonauts of the Western Atlantic, Bermuda's white settlers, produced a colorful history as seafarers for two and a-half centuries after the island's colonization in 1609. Adventure and risk were always present, as Bermuda lies in some of the world's most dangerous seas, separated by more than 600 miles from the nearest land. The more lucrative maritime activities, moreover, were either on the fringes of the law or well beyond it: piracy, privateering, wrecking, blockade running, smuggling. Yet these same pursuits, and those who earned distinction at them, have been romanticized in folklore and local histories, including one by a nun who, after 15 years in Bermuda, was so inspired by the tales of a legendary privateer and smuggler of the late eighteenth and early nineteenth centuries that she published a laudatory biography of him (Kennedy 1964).

The maritime period came to an end in the late nineteenth century, but the character values it encouraged—opportunism, daring, shrewdness, and so on—have been preserved in the economic culture of tourism and international finance, profitable but precarious industries built on high-risk, capital-intensive investment. The modern economy has also perpetuated a traditional notion of dependence on events and conditions in the outside world that can be exploited but not controlled. This outlook finds expression in the national motto: *"Quo Fata Ferunt*—Whither the Fates Lead Us."

The principal beneficiaries of Bermuda's prosperity have been a white oligarchy, who claim descent from the first British settlers, and who are known, not inappropriately, as the "Forty Thieves." Their relations to blacks, originally slaves and later a segregated underclass, have been paternal in the social and biological senses, creating an informal, personalized rapport that has coexisted with the institutional structures of racial separation (Parsons 1925). Predictably, the oligarchy's economic lifestyle has been influential among blacks, although it is typically articulated through symbols drawn from immediate black experience. Within the club milieu, for example, political and economic life is often described as a metaphorical sporting competition, and personal goals are sought through performative "game plans" built on calculated opportunism (Manning 1973: 87-147).

Gambling symbolizes an affinity between the swashbuckling adventurism of the white tradition and the black ethos of reputation. For all of their overt blackness, the stock market's "bad ass niggers" have an understanding of money and a style of relating to it that makes them potential allies of the white business class. The catalyst for developing this alliance has been party politics.

Challenged two decades ago by the emergence of a black political party, the white oligarchy responded by forming a coalition party of their own. They turned to both Anglo-whites of recent Bermudian ancestry, and to the Portuguese, who were rapidly gaining wealth in real estate, food merchandising, building construction, and other growing sectors. They also turned to blacks, coaxing them to cross the racial barrier with the promise of a generous "partnership" in the party and the expanding economy. In the early years of party politics, black partners were rewarded with jobs, political appointments, club memberships, and nominations to the Queen's Honor List. More recently, the benefits have escalated to include company directorships, blue ribbon investment opportunities, and, for those able to win elective seats, influential cabinet positions. The old obligarchy, who for centuries ran Parliament like a private club, have largely retired from the active political scene. But they continue to provide a major share of the party's enormous financial support which, more than anything else, has enabled it to enjoy an unbroken reign, and to frustrate the opposition's goal of black solidarity.

The stock market can be viewed as a caricature of the bi-racial power structure. The Portuguese gamblers are colorless but aggressive and successful entrepreneurs, while the blacks are flamboyant but dependent partners of white backers whose economic lifestyle bears striking affinities to their own. The parallel between gambling and politics is dramatized by the

With money tucked in his shorts, a gambler and his friend enter the stock market.

remarkable extent to which the black gamblers are active in the government party. Many of the table operators and known backers have run as candidates, whereas others have been campaign workers and financial supporters. One black table-operator was recently elected to the House of Assembly, and was formerly a government appointee to the Senate. Besides his role in the stock market he has been a major figure in the syndicates that run private crown and anchor parties, including the one involved in the celebrated court case cited earlier.

Talking to me on the street one day, a black table-operator explained his political leanings: "There is not one black person in Bermuda with any money who is PLP [the black opposition party]—not one.... If the white man looks after you, you've got to protect him." When an opposition supporter within earshot began to challenge him, the gambler yelled, "Shut the fuck up. It's niggers like you that are holding back motherfuckers like me."

As such exchanges indicate, gamblers and gambling are often at the center of partisan political controversy. The opposition party view the stock market as repugnant, to the extent that their committed supporters either stay away from it altogether or, at most, walk through without betting. The reason involves political distancing, of course, as well as an ideological judgement that gambling encourages consumerism and dependency and thus serves to keep blacks in a subordinate position. On a deeper level, however, the opposition's stance reflects black Bermudian religious culture, which is heavily influenced by evangelical Protestantism. From this standpoint, gambling is totally and unalterably sinful. The stock market, which couples gambling with other Protestant vices, such as drinking and sexual display, represents as radical a contrast as one could imagine to the type of social environment deemed suitable for one who is "saved."

Several years ago there was an attempt in the Bermuda House of Assembly to introduce a lottery to finance a sports stadium. The government party supported the bill, but gave members a free vote to mitigate the wrath of the black churches, which campaigned forcefully against it. The opposition party sided with the churches and unanimously opposed the bill (which was eventually defeated).

During the debate, a black member of the government party gave a supportive speech. He said that life was a matter of chance, and suggested that his honorable colleagues had been brought to the House by chance. He continued: "The main crux is that we have been living in a period of chance. We have been taking chances all our lives. I believe [the bill] might provide an opportunity to decide whether or not the community is prepared to take a national chance."

The speech was rebutted by an opposition member who is also a devout Pentecostal and the son of a preacher. "Life for me," he proclaimed, "is no gamble." He went on to contend that a "serpent" was responsible for the lottery legislation, and then linked gambling with alcohol and illicit sex. The proposed lottery, he concluded, would be the "thin edge of the wedge" in bringing "wholesale prostitution" to Bermuda.[5]

Countless other examples could be cited, but the point is simply that this sort of debate illustrates the extent to which partisan political division coincides with the fundamentalist opposition between sin and salvation. The opposition party has been partially successful in associating its cause with religious and moral symbols (Manning 1981 b), and there is no doubt that conservative Protestant norms are the ultimate value ideal of an overwhelming majority of black Bermudians. But temptation can be strong, particularly during festival time, when the lure of a quick dollar is hard to resist and other enticements of the gambling scenario are ambiguously licensed. The devil is active and persuasive here, as those who backslide from grace publicly attest.

As a social "text," the significance of the gambling scenario is twofold: it dramatizes the structure of power relations, and it shows the character and consequences of sin. Among blacks, there are few winners in the stock market. The players usually lose, and the table operators, although winning in the short run, are forced increasingly deeper into a position of clientage. They play attractive roles on stage, but they and their audience know that the script is written, directed and produced by their "partners." This is a powerful and unsettling political message in a culture that gives literal credence to the Pauline reminder, "The wages of sin is death."

Notes

[1]For a fuller discussion of festival cricket, see Manning 1981a.

[2]Bermuda's Gombey dancers are a localized version of the John Canoe mummering troupes found in Jamaica and, with variations, in many other Caribbean and circum-Caribbean countries.

[3]The Bermuda dollar is at parity with the U.S. dollar.

[4]A pseudonym.

[5]The legislative debate was reported in *The Royal Gazette,* 23 Feb., 1974, pp. 1, 2, 4.

Part IV

Masquerade Shows

Chapter 6

Carnaval in Rio: Dionysian Drama in an Industrializing Society

Victor Turner

Medieval European carnival had its roots in the pagan past with affinities to the Roman Saturnalia and Lupercalia. But it found a place in the calendar of the church year and was normally performed during the four days before Lent. Folk etymology connected carnival with the medieval Latin phrase "carne vale," (flesh farewell), since it marked a period of feasting and revelry just before Lent, when meat-eating fell under interdict. Being connected with a moveable fast, carnival—notably Mardi Gras—"Fat Tuesday," its climax, just before Ash Wednesay, became a moveable feast. Unlike such civic celebrations as Independence Day, July Fourth, *Cinco de Mayo,* and others, carnival is set in a cosmological calendar, severed from ordinary historical time, even the time of extraordinary secular events. Truly, carnival is the denizen of a place which is no place, and a time which is no time, even where that place is a city's main plazas, and that time can be found on an ecclesiastical calendar. For the squares, avenues, and streets of the city become, at carnival, the reverse of their daily selves. Instead of being the sites of offices and the conduits of purposive traffic, they are sealed off from traffic, and the millions who throng them on foot, drift idly wherever they please, no longer propelled by the urges of "getting and spending" in particular places.

What we are seeing is society in its subjunctive mood—to

borrow a term from grammar—its mood of feeling, willing and desiring, its mood of fantasizing, its playful mood; not its indicative mood, where it tries to apply reason to human action and systematize the relationship between ends and means in industry and bureaucracy. The distinguished French scholar, Jean-Richard Bloch, lamented in the title of his book, written in 1920, *Carnival est mort. Premiers essais pour mieux comprendre mon temps*, and the Spanish ethnologist Julio Caro Baroja, approvingly echoed him in 1965, "*el Carnaval ha muerto.*" "Carnival is dead," indeed! They said as much of pilgrimage when my wife and I set out to study this great mass phenomenon in 1970. We found that literally millions and millions of people were still on the pilgrimage trail of all the world's major religions, and, indeed, that many so-called "tourists" were really closet pilgrims. Certainly, *Carnaval* is by no means dead in Brazil, and rumors of its decease elsewhere are greatly exaggerated. One thinks immediately of Trinidad, New Orleans, and *Fastnacht* in many a German town.

But carnival, though a world-wide phenomenon—I am thinking of Japanese and Indian festivals such as the Gion *Matsuri* in Kyoto, or the *Holi* festival in northern India—has become in Brazil something fundamentally and richly Brazilian. I say this despite Brazilian criticism by certain middle-class elements that it is vulgar, by Marxists that it diverts the energies of the workers from political activity and blurs class lines, and by those in the higher clergy who look upon it as pagan and scandalous. The way people play perhaps is more profoundly revealing of a culture than how they work, giving access to their 'heart values.' I use this term instead of *key* values for reasons that will become clear, for the heart *has* its values, as well as its reasons.

The Varieties of Playful Experience

I am going to throw in a *soupcon* of theory into this *bouillabaisse* of carnivalesque impressions, since one of my recent concerns is the constant cross-looping of social history with the numerous genres of cultural performance ranging from ritual, to theatre, the novel, folk-drama, art exhibitions, ballet, modern dance, poetry readings, to film and television.

Underpinning each type of performance are the social structures and processes of the time; underlying the social drama or 'dramas of living,' the Dreyfus cases and Watergates, are the rhetorics and insights of contemporary kinds of performance—popular, mainstream and avant-garde. Each feeds and draws on the other, as people try to assign meaning to their behavior, turning it into conduct. They become reflexive, at once their own subject and object. One of the modes in which they do this is play—including games and sports, as well as festivals.

Play, paradoxically, has become a more serious matter with the decline of ritual and the contraction of the religious sphere in which people used to become morally reflexive, relating their lives to the values handed down in sacred traditions. The play frame, where events are scrutinized in the leisure time of the social process, has to some extent inherited the function of the ritual frame. The messages it delivers are often serious beneath the outward trappings of absurdity, fantasy, and ribaldry, as contemporary stage plays, some movies and some TV shows illustrate. Clearly, carnival is a form of play. Current theories of play formulated by anthropologists and others may give us some clues as to what carnival is about.

The main pioneer in this field is Dutch medieval historian Johan Huizinga, rector of the University of Leyden in 1933, and author of the celebrated book, *Homo Ludens* ("Man at Play," or "Man the Player"). Huizinga defined play as follows:

> Summing up the formal characteristics of play we might call it a free activity standing quite consciously outside 'ordinary life' as being 'not serious,' but at the same time absorbing the player intensely and utterly. It is an activity connected with no material interest, and no profit can be gained by it. It proceeds within its own proper boundaries of time and space according to fixed rules and in an orderly manner. It promotes the formation of social groupings which tend to surround themselves with secrecy and to stress their difference from the common world by disguise or other means (1955: 13).

Play, then, according to Huizinga, is a "free activity," which nevertheless imposes order on itself, from within and according to its own rules. He grasps the connection between play and the secret and mysterious, but cannot account for the fact that play is often spectacular, even ostentatious, as in parades, processions, Rose Bowls, Superbowls, and Olympics. One might even say that the masks, disguises and other fictions of some kinds of play are devices to make visible what has been hidden, even unconscious—for example, the Demon Masks of Sri Lankan and Tibetan exorcism rituals—to let the mysteries revel in the streets, to invert the everyday order in such a way that it is the unconscious and primary processes that are visible, whereas the conscious ego is restricted to creating rules to keep their insurgence within bounds, to frame them or channel them, so to speak. Huizinga is also surely wrong when he sees play as divested of all material interest. He forgets the important role of betting and games of chance in, for example, gambling houses, casinos, race tracks and lotteries. These may have important economic effects, even though playing for money remains completely unproductive, since the sum of the winnings at best only equals the losses of other players, and the entrepreneur, the bank, is the only ultimate winner; ironically he is perhaps the only one who takes no pleasure in gambling.

A later, more complex, theory of play has been developed by the French scholar, Roger Caillois. He uses some exotic terms, but defines them clearly. For example, he says that play has two axes or "poles," which he calls *paidia* and *ludus*. *Paidia*, from the Greek word meaning "child," stands for "an almost indivisible principle, common to diversion, turbulence, free improvisation, and carefree gaiety ... uncontrolled fantasy" (1979: 13). This anarchic and capricious propensity characteristic of children is countered by *ludus*, from the Latin word meaning "a play, a game," which Caillois sees as binding *paidia* "with arbitrary, imperative, and purposely tedious conventions, [opposing it] still more by ceaselessly practising the most embarrassing chicanery upon it, in order to make it more uncertain of attaining its desired effects" (*Ibid*). *Ludus*, in fact, represents how, in the space/time of the subjunctive mood of cultural action, human beings love to set up arbitrary obstacles to be overcome as in mazes, crossword puzzles or the rules of chess, which are both a general training for coping with obstacles in the day-to-day world and also a means of totally engrossing the player in a world of play framed and enclosed by its intricate rules.

Caillois has four additional concepts for understanding play (see Table 1, below). These are *agon*, Greek for "contest" or "competition"; *alea*, a dice game, extended to chance, randomness and gambling in general; mimicry, from the Greek *mimos*, an imitator or actor; and *ilinx*, for "whirlpool," which "consists of an attempt momentarily to destroy stability of perception and inflict a kind of voluptuous panic upon an otherwise lucid mind" (p. 23). Caillois uses these categories to explain the structure of games of strength, chance or skill, and of play-acting—all these being in the world of "make-believe" (whereas ritual is in the world of "we do believe").

Each category contains games and sports that move from the pole of *paidia*, childhood play (in which he includes "tumult, agitation, and immoderate laughter") to the pole of *ludus* ("purposive innovation"). For example, the category *agon* or competition describes a whole group of games "in which an equality of chances is artificially created in order that the adversaries should confront each other under ideal conditions, susceptible of giving precise and incontestable value to the winner's triumph.... Rivalry (usually) hinges on a single quality (such as speed, endurance, strength, memory, skill, ingenuity, and the like) exercised, within defined limits and without outside assistance, in such a way that the winner appears to be better than the loser in a certain category of exploits" (p. 14). Agonistic games range from unregulated racing and wrestling, at the *paidia* end, to organized sport (boxing, billiards, baseball, fencing, chess, Olympic Games, and so on) at the *ludus* end.

Alea or "chance" presides over "games that are based on a decision independent of the player, an outcome over which he has no control, and in which winning is the result of fate or destiny rather than triumphing over an adversary" (p. 17). For this reason, games of chance have often played an important role in ritual contexts, as indicative of the will of the gods, as in the great Indian epic, the *Mahabharata,* where the oldest of the *Pandava* hero-brethren gambles away the rights of all the brothers to the throne and to their joint wife Draupadi; the brothers pay the penalty of exile for thirteen years. In our culture, *alea,* chance, ranges from counting out rhymes (*eeny meeny miney mo*), and spinning a coin, at the *paidia* pole, to betting and roulette, to simple or complex continuing lotteries.

Mimicry or simulation involves the acceptance if not of an illusion (the very word is derived from the Latin *in-lusio*, "the beginning of a game"), at least of a "closed, conventional and, in certain respects, imaginary universe" (p. 19). Through mimicry one can become an imaginary character oneself, a subject who makes believe or makes others believe that he/she is someone other than him/herself. At the *paidia* pole, we have children playing at being parents or other adult roles, or cowboys and Indians, or spacemen and aliens. We progress through charades to various kinds of masking and costuming and disguises until at the *ludus* pole we are fully into theatre, masquerade, and, in the popular sphere, pageants, processions, parades, and other types of spectacle. Even the audience at great sports events, such as Superbowls, is under the spell of mimicry. The athletes who perform for them are dominated by *agon*, but for the audience, as Caillois writes, "A physical contagion leads them to assume the position of the contestants in order to help them, just as the bowler is known to unconsciously incline his body in the direction that he would like the bowling ball to take at the end of its course. Under these conditions, paralleling the spectacle, a competitive mimicry is born in the public, which doubles the *agon* of the field or track" (p. 22). This is easily observed in a crowd at a football or baseball game. Anticipating somewhat, we shall see how the two-by-four samba beat sweeps up watch the Rio *Carnaval* into mimicry of the *sambistas*, the members of the samba schools who compete with one another for the first prize in each year's glowing *Carnaval*.

The concept *ilinx* or vertigo involves all games which try to create disequilibrium or imbalance, or otherwise to alter perception or consciousness by inducing giddiness or dizziness, often by a whirling or gyrating motion. These range from such children's games as "Ring around the rosy," (Ashes, ashes, we all fall down!) and musical chairs to waltzing to horseriding to the intoxication of high speed on skis, water-skis, motorcycles, sports cars, to riding on roller-coasters, carousels, or other vertigo-inducing contraptions. Dancing comes under the sign of *ilinx*, as Caillois says, "from the common but insidious giddiness of the waltz to the many mad, tremendous, and convulsive movements of other dances" (p. 25). I would add, not least the samba! *Ilinx* shows that there is not only cosmos but chaos in the scheme of things.

Caillois sees an evolutionary development, as civilization advances in rationality from the unholy combination of mimicry and *ilinx*, which characterize the games and other cultural performances of societies he calls "primitive" or "Dionysian," which are ruled "by masks and possession"—to the rational sweetness and light of *agon* plus *alea*, represented by such "civilized" societies as the Incas, Assyrians, Chinese, and Romans. According to Caillois, these are "orderly societies with officers, careers, codes, and ready-reckoners, with fixed and hierarchical privileges, in which *agon* and *alea*, that is, merit and heredity (which is a kind of chance), seem to be the chief complementary elements of the game of living. In contrast to the primitive societies, these are 'rational' (p. 87).

Classification of Games

	Agon (competition)	Alea (chance)	Mimicry (Simulation)	Ilinx (Vertigo)
PAIDIA	Racing Wrestling etc. Athletics	Counting-out rhymes	Children's initiations Games of illusion	Children "whirling" Horseback riding
Tumult Agitation	(not regulated)	Heads or tails	Tag, Arms Masks, disguise	Swinging Waltzing
Immoderate laughter				
	Boxing, billiards	Betting		Volador
Kite flying	Fencing, checkers	Roulette		Traveling carnivals
Solitaire	Football, chess			Skiing
Patience				Mountain climbing
Crossword puzzles	Contests, Sports in general	Simple, complex, and continuing lotteries	Theatre Spectacles in general	Tightrope walking
LUDUS				

Note: In each vertical column games are classified in such an order that the *paidia* element is constantly decreasing while the *ludus* element is ever increasing.
Source: Roger Caillois, *Man, Play and Games* (1979).

Thus Caillois' scheme sees society solely from the positivist perspective of social structure, it fails to take into account the dialectical nature, which moves from structure to antistructure and back again to transformed structure; from hierarchy to equality; from indicative mood to subjunctive mood; from unity to multiplicity; from the person to the individual; from systems of status roles to *communitas,* the I-thou relationship, and Buber's "essential We" as against society regarded as "It."

Antonin Artaud understood at least this: that without a theater of mask and trance, of simulation and vertigo, the people perish—and this is as true of the most complex and large-scale society as it is of the most obscure aboriginal band. We would do well to value Caillois' conceptual analysis of play but avoid his evolutionist argument, for it disprizes the nonelitist societies that now have perhaps most to give to the general stream of human culture—rationality having ruined many of our natural resources in the name of procuring material comfort.

Great industrial nations such as Brazil and Japan have not despised their public festivals but elevated them to the scale of their secular achievements—all this without destroying the vertigo and theatricality at their liminal heart. We can learn much from their experience.

Aphrodite on the Half Shell

Perhaps the best way of approaching *Carnaval* is to consider how the Cariocas, the true inhabitants of Rio de Janeiro, describe it. Here is the first part of the lyric of a samba composed by the major *sambista* of the renowned Samba School, Estacao Primeira de Manguerira.

Quando uma luz divinal	When a light divine
Iluminava a imaginacao	Illuminated the imagination
De um escritor genial	Of a writer of genius
Tudo era maravilha	All was miracle
Tudo era seducao	All was seduction
Quanta alegria	How much happiness
E fascinacao	And fascination...
Relembro...	I remember
Aquele mundo encantado	That enchanted world

Fantasiado de doirado	Clad in the golden dress of fantasy
Oh! Doce ilusao	Oh! Sweet illusion [remember that illusion means 'entry into play]
Sublime relicario de crianca	Sublime shrine of childhood
Que ainda guardo como heranca	Which I still keep as a heritage
No meu coracao	In my heart

To savor this simple lyric one has to imagine it sung by a *puxador,* which means, surprisingly, a "puller". In *Carnaval* the word refers to a singer who rides ahead of an entire samba school on a float with a voice amplifier, pulling the school behind him, as it were. Some schools consist of many thousands of *sambeiros* who dance, mime, leap, gyrate, and sing choruses in his coruscating wake. He manages somehow to be at once stentorian and tender, tremendous and nostalgic, epic and romantic. His huge brazen voice is charged with *saudade,* an untranslatable Portuguese term, which is far more than the sum of "longing, yearning, ardent wish or desire, homesickness, affectionate greetings to absent persons, hankering for a lover or a homeland," as various Portuguese-English dictionaries describe the meaning.

The last few lines give the clue to a basic feature of *Carnaval.* It is propelled by *paidia* (childhood play). Freud once said that each of us is at once and successively a man, a woman and a child. The child is the player in us, and we are at times homesick for childhood's golden land, "sublime shrine of childhood, which I still keep as my heritage." Even the evident sexuality, the visible *libido,* of *Carnaval* has an infantine quality, like Beaudelaire's "paradis parfume." One could use, I suppose, such barbarous, infelicitous neologisms as "narcissistic display," "polymorphous perversion," and "fantasies about the primal scene," and so on, but this would be to endow the hummingbird lightness, deftness and butterfly-wing color of *Carnaval* play with a heavy northern seriousness, a puritanical spirit of gravity—"denaturing" it, some would say. Heaven help them!

The child is the epitome of antistructure, and perhaps this is why Jesus said, "Except ye become as little children, ye shall not enter the kingdom of heaven," the un-kingdom beyond social structure. One of the favorite types of *entitades*, as the invisible beings who incorporate themselves with mediums in such Brazilian cults as *Candomble* and *Umbanda* are called, is the line (*linha*) or legion of *criancas* (children). A medium possessed by a child-guide takes a diminutive name, Pedrinho, Joaozinho, and the like; speaks in a childish treble; and receives little treats such as candies from the congregation. The child-image is one link between Afro-Brazilian religious rituals which involve vertigo and trance, and *Carnaval* which involves mimicry, costuming and the enactment of a libretto or plot (*enredo*). Each samba school has its own plot, currently drawn by government edict from Brazil's patriotic past, a rule which makes it difficult but not impossible to slip in some sly digs at the generals' political preference. All this would make of *Carnaval* a "primitive" performance in Caillois' terms.

But we also find within the carnivalesque frame much *ludus* (complicated rules and regulations), *agon* (competition) and *alea* (chance and gambling). We see that the apparent and real 'childlike' is impregnated with a vast irony; the vertigo is tinctured by sophistication. *All* Caillois' components are sparking away furiously at once, like the plugs in a racing car or the wheels of Ezekial's chariot. We find that everything human is being raised to a higher power, the cognitive along with the emotional and volitional. For the spontaneity and freedom of *Carnaval* can *only* reach their uninhibited height in the four great days before Lent, *if* there has been a full year of organizing, plotting, and planning behind the scenes and a set of rules to channel the extravagant tide of song, dance, and generalized Eros.

Let us look at the growth of the samba schools in Rio and how they have been the response of an ever-young, ancient cultural genre to modernity. *Carnaval* has always been a many-levelled, as well as many-splendored, thing. Today there is not only the centrally organized street carnival of samba schools competing in leagues in downtown Rio and the internal carnival of the club balls on Mardi Gras itself, but there are also the locally organized processions of groups known as *blocos*, with their own songs and sambas, often subversive of the regime and not at all respecters of its persons. In addition, countless people dressed in their "private fantasies" stroll, flirt, get drunk and make love in streets and

A bikinied *mulata*, soul of the Rio *Carnaval*

squares from which business, commerce, and motorized traffic
have been summarily banished.

During *Carnaval,* those centers of Brazilian hierarchy—
the house, office, and factory—are emptied and closed. The
whole city becomes a symbol of Brazilianity, of a single
multicolored family brought into the open, which is
transformed into a home. *Carnaval* may, indeed, invade the
sacred homestead itself, as masked revellers swarm through it
and out again. Women, no longer under the *patria potestas* of
fathers or the *manus* of husbands, as in ancient Rome, become
the very soul of the samba in street and club. In a sense, the
whole city worships Aphrodite on the half-shell. Here
Aphrodite is a *mulata,* extolled in every song, and appearing in
person, in the tiniest of bikinis, on many a float, and revelling
with many a tamborinist in groups of two men and one woman,
known as *passistas.* The archetypal *mulata* was an eighteenth-
century 'lady,' Chica da Silva, who became a provincial
governor's mistress, and dominated men by her lambent, even
heroic, sexual prowess. Many movies and TV series have been
made about her.

Blacks and mulattos form the very core of *Carnaval,* since
they provide the central organization of every samba school,
while white celebrities clamor to be allowed into the *desfile,*
(pageant), as the total procession of *sambistas* and *sambeiros*
is called. The anthropologist, Roberto Da Matta, (in press),
calls this kind of organization, "a comet-like structure." The
permanent head of the comet is the *"Palacio do Samba",* the
large building located in a mainly black *favela* (slum),where
the organizing committee of the samba school has its offices—
a bureaucratic structure matching in complexity those of
government and business. It is also the site of intense
rehearsals which begin almost as soon as the previous
Carnaval is over. The floating "tail" of the comet consists of
the "one-day trippers" who wish to form part of the parade on
the Great Night and participate in its glory, together with , the
upper-class Brazilian *Brancos* (Whites) and foreign notables.
This type of grouping, which cuts across class and ethnic
divisions, Da Matta regards as typical of Brazilian social
organization. (The famous soccer clubs are similarly
organized.) It is encouraged, Da Matta argues, by the military
oligarchy ruling this hierarchical system, where, nevertheless,

uncontrollable industrial growth exerts a mounting pressure in the direction of liberalization, for aggressive, capitalistic business is hostile to red tape and rigid bureaucratic controls. It is clear that such comet-like structures regard the emergence of explicitly political groups with a single class basis, that is, political parties, contending with the establishment for real power and influence.

On the other hand, one might regard the samba school, with its multitudinous organizational problems and decisions made daily, as a school in governance and administration wherein countless blacks learn the skills of politics at the grass-roots level. And since a great samba school such as Manguera or Portela represents a sizeable constituency in itself, it can be expected to be wooed by local, even national politicians and administrators.

There is also an intimate connection between the leadership of Rio samba schools and the operators of the illegal kind of lottery known as *jogo do bicho*, a numbers game involving animal symbols. At the Niteroi *Carnaval* across the bay from Rio, my wife and I found ourselves, with Da Matta's help, in the mayor's box or cabin, along with novelist Jorge Amado. We discovered that a samba school had taken for its plot the entire body of Amado's work based on life in the state of Bahia, which always has a romantic glow for Brazilians, and dedicated its samba to him. The group in the box pointed out to me a number of "mobsters" who were deep in the numbers game, and who had contributed munificently to the expenses of the occasion and to particular samba schools. One of these took as its plot or theme "The Wheel of Fortune," with each of its segments, floats and samba libretto proclaiming the praises of Brazilian games of chance, cards, roulette wheels, *jogo do bicho*, betting on the races, and so on. One mobster was on the best of terms not only with dignitaries of the local government but also with officials and leading role-players of the samba schools as they passed the booths where their performances were given marks according to traditional criteria. Here is a clear association between competition and chance, *agon* and *alea*, in the parlance of Roger Caillois! As a matter of fact, Caillois himself remarked half-approvingly that "in Brazil gambling is king. It is the land of speculation and chance" (1979: 159).[1] Of course, the games/school link is

Gambling on parade in the Rio *Carnaval*

pragmatic as well as symbolic, and many cultural connections are at once instrumental and expressive, and symbols arising in a "play world" are often manipulated to serve political interests and purposes.

If one could say that "antistructure" were merely vertigo and mimicry, one could agree with Maria Goldwasser at the University of Rio de Janeiro when she describes "the crystallization of antistructure," the basic idea which explained for her the functioning of the Mangueira samba school.

> Antistructure is represented here by Carnaval, and is defined as a transitional phase in which differences of (pre-Carnaval) status are annulled, with the aim of creating among the participants a relationship of *communitas*. Communitas is the domain of equality, where all are placed without distinction on an identical level of social evaluation, but the equivalance which is established among them has a ritual character. In *communitas* we find an inversion of the structured situations of everyday reality marked by routinization and the conferment of structural status. The status system and communitas—or structure and antistructure (which also possesses its own systematic character)—confront one another as two homologous series in opposition.
>
> The carioca Carnaval is the exemplary representation of antistructure. 'To make a Carnaval' is equivalent 'to making a chaos,' where everything is confused and no-one knows where anything is. In Carnaval, men can dress as women, adults as babies, the poor as princes and, even more, 'what means what' becomes an open possibility by a magical inversion of real statuses and a cancellation or readjustment of the barriers between the social classes and categories. (1975:82-3).

Yet Goldwasser found that Mangueira, or *"Old Manga,"* the name by which the school is everywhere known, is complicatedly organized and structured. She presents a chart of the organization which resembles that of a major firm or government department. Briefly, it is divided into the directory of the school, whose function is mainly administrative, and the *Carnaval* commission, which operates in the artistic realm. The first is subdivided into three parts: (1) the Wing of the Composers (of the year's main samba and other musical items which deal with the technical supplies and emoluments of the composers themselves; (2) the Wing of the Battery, divided again between artistic and administrative spheres; the *bateria* is the awe-inspiring, compact mass of drummers and other percussion instrumentalists who bring up the rear of a samba school; by law, only percussion instruments can be used in a school's grand parade on the second day of *Carnaval;* some schools are known for their *bateria* which earns them high marks from the judges. Then there is (3) the Committee of the Combined Wings, whose job is to integrate the numerous components of the school's parade. Under the battery officials are the *ritmistas*, the drummers themselves, who are also partly organized by the composers' officials. The *puxadores* and "crooners" also come under the wing of the composers.

In addition to this pattern of technical control, there is a parallel hierarchy in the artistic sphere which attends to such matters as overall design, the plot or libretto and its apportionment among the various components of the parade: the synchronization of dance, song, music, and miming; the tastefulness of the whole presentation; the designing and decoration of floats, costuming and coiffeuring, and the rest. It takes a great amount of order to produce "a sweet disorder," a great deal of structuring to create a sacred play-space and time for antistructure. If "flowing"—*communitas* is "shared flow"—denotes the holistic sensation when we act with total involvement, when action and awareness are one, (one ceases to flow if one becomes aware that one is doing it), then, just as a river needs a bed and banks to flow, so do people need framing and structural rules to do their kind of flowing. But here the rules crystallize out of the flow rather than being imposed on it from without. William Blake said a similar thing using the metaphor of heat: "Fire finds its own form." This is not dead structure, but living form; Isadora Duncan, not classical ballet. The "structure" described by Goldwasser is akin to the rules of sport, and belongs to the domain of *ludus*, not to the politico-economic order.

The Palace of Carnaval

The competition between samba schools, indeed their very existence in their present form, is a fairly recent *Carnaval* phenomenon. The first school, named *Deixa Falar* ("Let 'em talk"), was formally constituted on 12 August, 1928 in Estacio, a city ward which was—and still is—a traditional stronghold of *Carnaval*. Until about 1952, according to de Moraes (1958), *Carnaval* was a rather brutal revel, the heir of the Portuguese *entrudo* (Shrovetide), chiefly consisting of a vulgar battle in which pails of water were thrown about indiscriminately at people in the streets and plazas. Such customs die hard, for I saw fraternity brethren doing exactly the same thing, at the University of Minnesota during the University Carnival! My wife saw Cambridge University students doing this in the 1930s on Shrove Tuesday. The wide diffusion of similar carnival customs is perhaps due first to the spread of the Roman Empire which introduced such anti-structural rites as *Saturnalia* and Lupercalia to its distant provinces, and secondly to the spread of the Catholic Church which took with it around the world not only a common liturgy and liturgical year, but also a host of popular feasts and customs representing in some cases 'baptised' circum-Mediterranean pre-Christian rituals.

Entrudo drenching was banned by an edict of 1853 and there succeeded a number of new forms of merrymaking. The popular inventiveness of *Carnaval* is limitless; a constant mutation in the type and scope of the revels abounds. Space prohibits mentioning most of them, but one should note the *rancho* of the early 1900s, a group of masqueraders which included a band and a chorus, specializing in the so-called *marchas-rancho*, which have a markedly slow cadence in *choros*, a sentimental musical form, and later in sambas. The *ranchos* opened up the carnival to young women. Their costumes became richer and more luxurious, with a profusion of silks, velvets, spangles, plumes, and sequins. Usually the *ranchos'* names were rather flowery: "Flowery of the Avocado," "Solace of the Flowers," "Pleasurable Mignonette."

But in the twenties and thirties the tempo of life changed and the young rejected the sugariness of the *rancho* style, desiring a lighter and different flow of rhythm and shorter, less elaborate lyrics. The samba came into its own, and the units that played it were, first, the *blocos*, and soon after, the samba schools. *Bloco* is a genus, applying originally to any informal group of carnival participants, usually from the lower and humbler social strata.[2] In the film *Dona Flora and Her Two Husbands* the carnivalesque first husband had a fatal heart attack while dancing in a *bloco*. A species of this genus is the *bloco de sujos* ("bloc of the dirty ones"), designating either a loosely organized band of ragamuffins, or a group of revelers that paint their faces with charcoal and rouge and dress in loud colors in artless fashion. These groups have a chaotic, disarrayed appearance, and seem to portray best the "vertigo" component of carnival play. Another species is called *bloco de arrastao* ("bloc of the fishing net"), for as the group moves along, the seduction of its rhythmic chanting and the dancing of its members prove irresistible to spectators, who, totally unable to resist, are "pulled in" to sing and dance.

Hundreds of *blocos* still exist in Rio. They rejoice in such names as *Vem Amor* ("Do Come, Love"), *Vai Quem Quer* ("Come Who Will"), *Namorar Eu Sei* ("In Loving, I Know"), *Suspiro da Cobra* ("Sigh of a Snake"), *Canarios das Laranjeiras* ("Canaries from Larenjeiras"—a ward of Rio), and *Bloco do Gelo* ("Ice Block"). New *blocos* come into being with each carnival, while older ones disappear. What usually happens is a that a large and well-organized *bloco* eventually establishes a samba school. Like the schools, large *blocos* have detailed regulations and by-laws, are governed by a board of directors, democratically elected by all the members at a general assembly, have adopted heraldic colors of their own, and appear at carnival time wearing uniform costumes which have been especially made for the occasion. Lastly, some of the better-off *blocos*—like the major samba schools—are the proprietors of the clubhouse where they have their headquarters and of the place where they hold their rehearsals.

The samba schools are organized into three leagues, with demotion of the last two schools in the first and second leagues and promotion of two schools from the second and third to replace them. An awards committee judges them. Although their numbers fluctuate, informants suggest that there are now nine jurors. One evaluates the guild's flag, since each "school" is officially a guild (*gremio*) and the line of its officials is known as the *comissao de frente*, usually numbering fifteen, who march at the head of the parade, often in frock coats and top hats. The second evaluates the performance of the flag-bearer, the *porta-bandeira*, and the major-domo, or *mestre-*

sala; usually the flag-bearer is the most beautiful woman of the school and the best dancer—always she appears in the dress of an eighteenth-century lady. At every carnival the school presents a different, beautifully embroidered flag, showing on one side the emblem of the guild and on the other some design indicating the plot which is presented in that particular pageant. Until 1967 the flag itself was awarded points, but not subsequently. The major-domo is also called *baliza*, literally a signpost or landmark. This is apt for he is really the pivot round which the choreography revolves. He is usually tall and slim, agile and graceful. He appears either in seventeenth-century attire, with short cape and plumed hat—like one of Dumas' musketeers—or in the silk and satin knee-length coat of the eighteenth century, with powdered wig in the style of Louis XV. He carries a small fan in his left hand, or a lace handkerchief, and with his right he holds his partner's hand or her waist, as the dance may require. They dance together and then separate. She then gyrates swiftly, the silk of the flag sighs as it cuts the air, while he dances round her, inventing complicated steps, kneeling, bowing as gracefully and delicately, as if he were in Versailles in the days of Louis-le-Beinaime. While these blacks from the poor slums display the elegance of a vanished feudalism in their liminality, the white 'beautiful people' in the restricted indoor *Carnaval of the Clubs* revert to the almost naked barbarism of the night revels of the *La Dolce Vita*. Whites dress down, and blacks dress up.

The third judge evaluates the school's current plot and the lyrics of the samba, which always refer to the plot and indeed create its emotional tone. The fourth judge evaluates the appearance of the school as a whole and the choreography of the ensemble: the main components are the *alas*, (wings), consisting of 10 to 30 persons, often of the same sex, who are organized around a subplot, which must conform to the school's main plot. In addition to the *alas*, there are the *destaques* or *figuras de destaque*, "the stand-outs" or individual items. These are persons wearing sumptuous and magnificent costumes and plumes, who strut down the avenue in solitary, solar, lunar, or rainbow splendor. Quite often, they are transvestites, with silicon implants to caricature femininity, and commonly well-known Rio socialites. Floats are also a carnival component, limited by regulation to four per school, including the float that spearheads the pageant, known as the *abre-alas* (literally "wings-opener or usher"). Its purpose is to proclaim the name of the school and the title of its plot for the year. An *abre-alas* may represent an open book, a large portal, or a baroque cartouche (like those that appear in old maps and charts). By tradition, the text used is as follows: "G.R.E.S. [an acronym for Gremio Recreativo Escola de Samba Mangueira) or pays its compliments to the people of Rio, presents [here follows the plot's title], and requests permission to pass through." Some of the floats are unbelievable. It is recorded that the *Portela* school, in 1965, exhibited a float that was an exact replica of the library of Princess Isabel in which she signed the Act of Abolition of Slavery! (Another example of black Brazilian elegance). Some floats are in rank bad taste, however, and some schools have substituted for them painted panels and screens and a series of *gonfalons* (standards with two or three streamers) and *oriflammes* (red silk banners split at one end) carried by members of the school.

The fifth judge evaluates the tunefulness and musical texture of the samba and the performance of the *bateria*. The number of bandsmen may vary greatly. The incomparable *bateria* of the *Academicos de Cubango* took the avenue by storm at the *Carnaval* I attended. We were all swept away on the great tide of the samba played on drums by hundreds of *ritmistas*. As mentioned earlier, only percussion instruments are permitted, but they include large and small drums such as *cotixa*, the military drum, and many others; friction drums (*cuicas*) which can make several sounds at once in syncopation; *agogos*, derived from African hunting bells; tambourines; *pandeiros* or timbrels; polished saucepans; and many more. The smaller instruments are played by *passistas*, dexterous leapers and contortionists, who often cavort, two men to one girl, in the sexiest of postures. We all fell in behind the *ritmistas* and *passistas* in a Dionysiac abandonment I have never experienced before or since.

What is it like to be a *sambista* or *sambeiro*? One journalist, Sergio Bitencourt, writing in the *Correio da Manha*, claims that the *Carnaval* is "a mission, a mandate, a supreme moment of deliverance and self-sufficiency." He adds: "The drops of perspiration which cover the face of the *sambista* have the savor of drops of blood." Here we have what Huizinga calls "the deep earnestness in play," even a hint of the *Via Dolorosa, the Way of the Cross. Festival, at times, is not too far from its ritual origins and can give its participants something akin to a religious experience—Ash Wednesday is not too far behind Mardi Gras. Death is implicitly present; in the movie *Black Orpheus* he appeared in the guise of *Exu* of the cemeteries, the chaos deity of the *Umbanda* religion. *Exu sem Luz.*

The sixth juror evaluates the masquerades and the individual floats. Their mimicry is magnificently complex. No anthropologist has yet done an adequate study, either aesthetic or semiotic, of the costumes, masks, disguises, ritual nakedness, color symbolism, and the structural oppositions and meditations among all these, that can be found in any Rio carnival.

To round off my tally of the jurors, three are placed at different locations on the parade route to assign negative votes as penalties for any delays caused by willful negligence. There is further anthropological material in the politicking that surrounds the awards committee, and the hostility, often leading to violence—even homicide and suicide—which greets their final assessment of the various schools' performances. The jurors are drawn from the ranks of professional artists or art critics; dress designers; newspaper persons; television personnel; professional ballet dancers, choreographers, musicians, and composers. But umpires and referees are seldom popular in any of the fields of play we have been talking about. When play makes serious statements about the human condition, people take its outcomes seriously.

It is a Brazilian point of honor that if one is going to wear a costume, or *fantasia*, it must communicate one's most private or intimate fantasy in the most artistic way possible. Repression must be lifted. One might even talk about the aestheticization of the repressed, making the very private very public in the mode of beauty. The secret of Brazilian culture perhaps lies in this, that it has created a "palace of *Carnaval*," a place of samba, out of fantasies suppressed through the rest of the year by immersion in industrial labor, by submission to an autocratic regime, by tenacious vestiges of feudal attitudes in the relations between men and women, young and old. Even more, Brazilian culture has raised a traditional ritual of reversal to the scale of a great industrial nation, in every way equivalent, in its subjunctive mood and at the unconscious and preconscious levels, to the complex modern industrial nation that is Brazil's indicative mood and conscious reality. *Carnaval* is made to serve as a kind of paradigm, or model, for the whole modern and post modern world. *Carnaval* is no Aldous Huxleyan "orgy porgy," for its ironical, whimsical, urbane, and genial touch dispels such a thought. Rather it is the creative anti-structure of mechanized modernity. *Carnaval* is the reverse of fiction or fake: it demands validity of feeling, sad or glad. It is mostly glad, and there is no mistaking the authenticity of radiant joys that pour out of faces and songs, and make the samba live up to one of its names, *arrasta-pe* (netter or snarer of feet). No one can feel embarrassed in the many-dimensioned world of carnival. "Shame is absent from *Carnaval*," the saying goes. It is a world oblivious of original sin, as its own lyrics dare to say in a Christian country... *Aquele mundo encantado* ("that enchanted world"). The Golden Age really does return. Naturally, there are many Brazilians who are skeptical, regarding *Carnaval* as "opium for the people" (though 'speed' would perhaps be a better metaphor). Again, at *Carnaval* time the roads leading from Rio are choked with the cars of the middle class, fleeing the revelries of the streets, dreading the carnivalesque reversal of their hard-won bourgeois values.

What has Caillois and his theories of play to do with all this? Only that *Carnaval* engulfs all his categories in a dynamic, many-levelled, liminal domain of multiframed anti-structures and spontaneous *communitas*. *Paidia, ludus, agon, alea*, mimicry and *ilinx* are spun together indistinguishably in the spangled tapestry of the nocturnal parade of the Carioca samba schools. As the poet, Cassiano Ricardo, put it: A bit of Brazil in the hearts of angry men—wouldn't it be a solution?"

Notes

1An article in the *Los Angeles Times* (10 May, 1981) discloses how in 1975 the wealthy Rio *banquiero*, Anix Abrahao David, "took over the Beija Flor samba school (holder of a record three first-place trophies), and pumped hundreds of thousands, if not millions, of dollars into the operation."

2Julie Taylor informs me that today there seems to be a resurgence of 'spontaneous' *Carnaval*, in protest against commercial celebrations, both by humbler and middle-class strata. These contemporary *blocos* are particularly typical of the latter, if not of both.

Chapter 7

The Shit Devil:
Pretense and Politics Among
West African Urban Children

Jeanne Cannizzo

In most of the anthropological literature, the child is of interest only for what an examination of its nature might reveal about adult society, for these studies present the child as a rather passive recipient whose world only reflects adult culture (Hardman 1973). Much of the literature is on child-rearing practices or socialization; there are very few studies that "report on what children see as they observe the world in which they find themselves" (Goodman 1970:2).

Yet there is clearly a case to be made for an anthropology of children—their beliefs and values, oral traditions, folklore and rituals, and world view; there is a culture of childhood. It is hoped that my paper on a children's art form will contribute to the ethnography of children. My focus on street masquerading, which will hopefully further our understanding of the culture of childhood, is based on Fernandez' premise that "culture is aesthetic preference drawn large" (1973: 194). Other authors have treated this theme and have expressed the same sentiments in somewhat different form. Geertz, in considering Balinese cockfighting as "deep play," suggests that:

> ... cultural forms can be treated as texts, as imaginative works built out of social materials.... Art forms generate and regenerate the very subjectivity they pretend only to display. Quartets, still lifes, and cockfights are not merely

reflections of a pre-existing sensibility analogically represented; they are positive agents in the creation and maintenance of such a sensibility. (1972: 27-28).

The present study focuses on the *Alikali* devils (the generic term for child-maskers) sponsored by urban associations of young schoolboys in Bo, Sierra Leone. These masking groups—multi-ethnic, residentially based, segregated by sex but not religion or social status—are composed of seven or eight boys aged eight to twelve. This membership pays a subscription fee, used to construct a devil (masquerade), which will perform publicly on the main streets of town during the major Muslim or Christians festivals.

Devildom and Boyhood

There are four devil types—the Rainbow, the *Talabi*, the Jolly and the *Kaka*—which can be viewed respectively as three champions or heroes of childhood and one clown. The Jolly devil, acrobatic artist supreme, as he leaps and somersaults his way down the road, embodies that most remarkable, if transitory, trait of the immature—their vitality; the Rainbow devil is "Beauty," enshrined and festooned in expensive, imported Christmas tinsel and silk veils. The horned *Talabi* is the paladin of power, an aggressive masker who attacks the adult world with impudent tricks. It is, however, the *Kaka* devil (the faeces or "shit" devil) that is of concern here, for it is a rather easily recognized but an interesting example of symbolic inversion.[1]

The contrariness of the *Kaka* is immediately apparent in its costume, for the cloth is old, dirty (literally), and torn. These attributes of the *Kaka* ensemble are selected for the signifying song of this particular type of masquerade: *Kaka devil boss trousers* ("boss"—burst or torn). The second line of this theme song, *Ah de fall down* also comments on a reversal of normal devil behavior; the *Kaka* throws himself into the dust of the streets and rolls over and over causing the dust to settle on himself as well as on the spectators. That the *Kaka* masker participates in the choral accompaniment to his own dance and the vocal expose, coupled with the fact that his costume is not intact, makes it clear that this devil is a human being dressed up in a costume. When asked to describe a *Kaka* devil, boys most commonly commented *e no fine* ("it isn't fine").

To be fine, a most desirable state for a Rainbow, Jolly or *Talabi*, and a state that the *Kaka* cannot achieve, is to be three things: costly, bright and new. Brightness and expensiveness are worthless, and in fact unattainable, without newness—in the sense not of novelty but of perfect condition. A really fine devil dress is not torn, old, smelly or dirty. A costume that becomes so is discarded because *e don poil* ("it has spoiled"); it is this appreciation and expectation of the perfect that makes the *Kaka* the antidevil, for by deliberately violating the standards of excellence laid down for masquerading, it embodies the ugly.

It is, of course, not uncommon in West African societies for the dialogue between the beautiful and the ugly to be given physical form in masquerades, and the *Kaka* as aesthetic inversion and antidevil has parallels in adult masquerades in Sierra Leone. But the *Kaka* devil, and indeed his companions, the Jolly, Rainbow and *Talabi*, are not miniature models of adult masquerades that contribute only to the continuity of the artistic traditions of which they are copies. Those aspects of cultural and social behavior that children acquire within the context of participation in an adult festival are not generated within the peer group, but occur under the aegis of the adult society. The *Alikali* devils, however, are independent creations, art forms which are produced by and for children, and in contradiction to the Krio[2] proverb which suggests disapprovingly that "a child who does not learn his lesson from his mother will be trained on the street." There are some things which are well learned on the street, things a boy cannot learn from his mother. Certain financial talents, politico-judicial skills, sexual stereotypes, and values are acquired by the boys in their masking associations through socialization and enculturation within the peer group.

In some ways the boys, although independent of adult supervision, train themselves to see the world as adults see it, to "interpret their present and future roles in very much the same ways as their parents have done" (Mayer and Mayer 1970: 162). The conservatism of boys in Bo is sometimes striking; for example, most boys hold the same stereotypic views of feminine nature as do grown men and, like men, live in

Accompanied by "pan" music, a horned *Talabi* devil does an energetic dance.

sexually segregated social worlds. Any such similarities are not surprising when it is borne in mind that there are other avenues of socialization, under adult supervision, besides that of the peer group: the family (natal or otherwise, as some children are boarders or guests in the homes of relatives while attending school), the schools, and the men's secret societies. However, caution must be exercised in ascribing to these institutions too much of a levelling effect. The boys in *Alikali* associations attend Christian, Ahmadiyya, Koranic, and nonsectarian schools, all of which promote the attainment of somewhat different social skills and attitudes, and come from families where child-rearing practices vary greatly.

It may be that these institutions foster differences in the orientations and world views of the boys that must, to some extent, be overcome if they are to enjoy the full benefits accruing to them from their participating in a masking association. In fact, whereas in some respects the boys' *Alikali* groups are conservative, in others they are radical; that is, they hold views and expectations that depart from those held by the adults around them. This is, in part, because the boys operate most fully within the modern social environment of the town, for they are not only urban children, but in many cases very urbane ones. In contrast, although a few adults in Bo operate almost totally within the framework of the more traditional system of status, and others confine themselves almost wholly to participation in the modern achievement system, the majority of adults, particularly men, live their lives within both systems.

Many urban dwellers retain a degree of commitment to status systems, values and attitudes that govern social relationships in rural villages. But in other ways, these same men and women are part of an achievement-oriented society, for:

> ... the substitution of a market economy for an economy based upon subsistence involved the disturbance of traditional ideas of status, new roles are created whose fulfillment necessitates the interaction of individuals on a basis of common interest in such things as wages, education, religion, and politics rather than genealogical origin and descent (Little 1970: 1).

Whether achieved or ascribed, "traditional" or "modern," these status systems divide the adult world of Bo into many separate strata or spheres, and although it may be misleading to state that in their masking associations, children resolve some of the conflicts that disturb the harmony of the parental generation, it can be suggested with some assurance, that children dissolve some of the boundaries that confine adults to particular spheres. Whatever the conflicts within the *Alikali* groups, they are not generated by the same rivalries and prejudices governing the social relationships of men and women. For, it will be recalled, the boys do not limit their groups to those of a particular social class, ethnic group, religion, or educational background—*all* boys within the street and neighborhood are asked to join. The world the boys create within their associations is an egalitarian one. The patterns of membership indicate the boys' subscription to, if not vocalization of, a philosophy dedicated to removing the inequalities and artificialities of the world of men. Nor are the hierarchies of that world perpetuated after the formation of the association, for within these groups the social process is not statified but charismatic.[3]

Leadership, whether it be political or in performance, is based on *personal* qualities—mental and emotional, physical, intellectual, and creative—for the boys inhabit a meritocracy where appointments and promotions are based on competence, where individual boys demonstrate their skills and abilities as superior to those of their fellows. These are not achieved or ascribed attributes; they are talents, the natural endowments of a person, and as such are rather different from the *impersonal* achievements of the urban world where (at least in Bo) educational success, promotion and even choice of employment, membership in societies, and the like are still often gained by means of one's ascribed status.

It is thus obvious that the groups are radical in their departure from adult orientations, but the *Alikali* devil groups are *not* rebellious; they do not "challenge expectations of the parent culture" (Mayer and Mayer 1970: 183). They do not defy adult standards and values, or outrage public (that is, adult) opinion with criminal or delinquent acts, later to renounce these ideals and return to the 'family' of adults as prodigal sons.

If the devil groups are not rebellious, they *are*, however, revolutionary in that they affect not merely a change of social personnel but also a change of social structure. For the masking associations represent the members of a new institution, or, to use Cohen's phrase, they are "the formal expression of an informally organized interest group." In *Two Dimensional Man*, Cohen suggests that.

> ... societies consist of a multiplicity of interest groups of all sizes and sorts that quarrel, compete, federate, crosscut, and overlap with one another, to protect and increase their share of power. These are thus essentially political groupings and their activities determine the distribution, maintenance, and exercise of power in society (1974: 65).

The members of these interest groups are engaged in a struggle to define the limitations, rights and obligations, the assets and liabilities of a new estate; they are engaged in the *politics of childhood*. The politics of childhood are the politics of identity and in many ways the masking associations resemble tribal associations that are, of course, interest groups with political functions. Tribal associations institutionalize ambiguity and "grapple with all the unresolved issues of change—how people of different languages are to relate to each other, how their traditions are to merge in a nation, how family loyalties are to be reconciled with loyalty to the state" (Marris 1974:92).

The *Alikali* associations themselves, the values they promote, the art forms they sponsor, the *lingua franca* (Krio) with which they communicate amongst themselves, all are the trappings of a new collective identity, for the boys have invented, where none existed before, a new 'tribe'—of children. Why should the forging of such an 'ethnic identity' be necessary, and what are the artistic mechanisms by which this new identity is displayed in symbolic form?

The Creation of Children

Children as *children* are a new feature of the Sierra Leonean cultural life and social structure. Following the argument of Phillipe Aries (1962) on the development of the concept of childhood in European society, it can be suggested that this institution of childhood, as it is popularly and currently perceived, is of modern origin. Not only is childhood a recent phenomenon, but it is associated with the rise of the nuclear family and the schools that, in their turn, are primarily, in West Africa, aspects of urban life.

Aries, beginning his analysis in the Middle Ages, suggests that in:

> ... medieval society the idea of childhood did not exist; this is not to suggest that children were neglected, forsaken or despised. The idea of childhood is not to be confused with affection for children: it corresponds to an awareness of the particular nature of childhood, that particular nature which distinguishes the child from the adult, even the young adult. In medieval society this awareness was lacking....
>
> As soon as he had been weaned, or soon after, the child became the natural companion to the adult. They immediately went straight into the great community of men, sharing in the work and play of their companions, old and young alike.
>
> Transmission from one generation to the next was ensured by the everyday participation of children in adult life (1962: 128, 411, 368).

Anthropological data on children in Sierra Leone is limited to those adult activities, such as naming rituals and child-rearing practices, in which children are the focal point. However, the few descriptions of childlife in rural villages indicate that here too the child is little separated from adult life, that many of its activities not only contribute to, but are, indeed, mirror images of adult actions:

> Special technological skills are usually learnt by an apprenticeship system whereby young children live with and work for a craftsman while learning the trade from him in return. All children will have seen blacksmiths at work, houses and fences being constructed and furniture made and all will at least have some knowledge about distillation of liquor, the use of cement, how bicycles work, boat building and the expressing of palm oil.
>
> They learn about their own society, the history of their family and village by listening to stories and historical accounts by elders on the veranda in the evenings and the elders look upon it as their duty to do so.
>
> As the child grows up he or she is expected to perform

various duties. Young boys and girls are expected to help in the kitchen with the more monotonous tasks such as washing and pounding rice. Young boys have to carry water and look after sheep, and young girls to sweep the yard. As they grow up their tasks become more distinct as they assume their respective sex roles as exemplied, par excellence, in farming operations where women weed the farm, bring food and clean threshed rice, whereas young boys are soon employed with digging and harvesting (Peace Corps n.d.).

The important distinctions between people and the divisions within the rural societies from which the families in Bo ultimately derived were those between freemen and slaves, 'chiefly' and commoner families, male and female initiate and non-initiate. Throughout, education promoted the passage of an individual through partial to full participation in adult society.

New ideas on child care and the perception of the child as a dependent did, of course, reach West Africa from Europe, but they are not intrinsically 'Western,' since in Europe these ideas and conceptions began to gain currency only in the seventeenth century. During this century, not only is the concept of the child absent, but the nuclear family, although obviously a physical reality, tends to be socially invisible. It was the extended kinship group, which Aries calls the "line," that formed the basic conception of a family during the Middle Ages.

As is readily apparent upon any visit to a Sierra Leonean village, life is as public here as it was in earlier European societies, for most of it takes place out of doors in the village meeting-place or in front of family compounds. All of the extremes, as well as the continuities, of social intercourse are visible to the general crowd of men, women, children, neighbors, and kinsmen with whom, so intimately, one's life is shared. Here, too, the nuclear family is of lesser significance, for wider kinship connections provide the structure upon which many interpersonal relationships rest.

There are, then, important parallels between rural, traditional Sierra Leonean society and that of medieval Europe and then, in the easy access across age barriers and integration of the young and the old, in the importance of the extended, as opposed to the nuclear, family, and the publicity of daily life.

Gradually, however, a concept of childhood emerges during the Middle Ages, which manifests itself in various ways. For example, children were seen to have a particular nature, distinct from that of adults, and in the sixteenth and seventeenth centuries they acquired their own special clothes, games, and so on. Adults became more interested in the "moral welfare and development" of their children and began to "subject them to a thoughtful and rigorous regime designed to help inculcate self-control, to shield them from the immodesties of adult life, and to treat them with seriousness" (Hunt 1970:34).

Changes in educational precepts and practices were occurring as well, not only paralleling but promoting changes in family structure and the concept of the child. During the Middle Ages most children were simply apprenticed to adults from about the age of seven. Although schools existed, they were institutions devoted to the teaching of Latin, without the benefit of any ideas relating curriculum to age, for schoolboys were regarded as adults. Students often formed *corps*, within which associations the pupils were led by leaders of their choice who enforced rules made by the students themselves. They were simply members of one of the many independent units of society.

> The school ceased to be confined to clerics and became the normal instrument of social initiation, of progress from childhood to manhood...
> [this change] corresponded to a desire on the part of the parents to watch more closely over their children, to stay nearer to them, to avoid abandoning them even temporarily to the care of another family. The substitution of school for apprenticeship likewise reflects a rapprochement between parents and children, between the concept of the family and the concept of childhood, which had hitherto been distinct. The family centered itself on the child. Family and school together removed the child from adult society (Aries 1962: 269, 413).

The modern family, originally a middle-class phenomenon, also removed itself from the rest of society so that it became a discrete group of parents and children, with the energy of the group expended on the children and their individual rise in the world (Aries 1962: 404).

The historical developments outlined above were, of course, gradual ones, so that at any point in time, some families and some children were at different places on the social continuum. Urban families in Sierra Leone also currently exhibit a wide variety of familial structures and child-rearing practices, as well as expectations regarding modern education. But all the evidence points not only to the growing numbers, in fact now a majority, of monogamous households in urban areas, but also to the growing influence and importance of the nuclear family (Gamble 1963; Kaplan 1976). In addition, all of these families wish to educate their male children, and so the child is synonymous with the schoolboy. However, education most often separates the child from his parents. It has been suggested by Sutton-Smith that the scientific revolution in knowledge further segregated the child from knowledge:

> Differentiation of knowledge...meant reality was no longer the same for all men. There were various canons of truth. Men could no longer make judgements in confidence and in terms of immediate perceptual information. The affairs and understandings of adults became increasingly invisible to children. As a result children were, in fact, increasingly innocent. (1972: 304)

In Sierra Leone, where 75 to 80 percent of the adult population is illiterate, the situation is, in a sense, reversed. The affairs and understandings of children become increasingly invisible to adults, for the boys' modern education ensures that there are currently at least two canons of truth, one mature, and one immature in terms of age, if not in knowledge, of the modern world. The schoolboy is, however, increasingly dependent on his parents and family in a different way, for although his labor no longer makes a significant contribution to the family income, the family must provide his school fees and textbooks, and annual tuition. As this dependency increasingly excludes boys from the world of men, they begin to create a children's world, where adults are excluded, and where they themselves are independent.

Status Reversal

The *Alikali* devils exist because their creators are no longer infants but not yet men; they are not yet among the initiated. But to categorize them as the uninitiated would no longer be an apt or adequate description, for these mask-makers and mask-wearers are *children*. As such, within the particular contextual environment of the Sierra Leonean town of Bo, they occupy a structurally weak and ill-defined position, for childhood is as yet an anomalous and ambiguous institution, one which is still emerging. As members of this estate, the boys are liminal *personae* whose comradeship within their masking associations joins them in childish *"communitas"* (Turner 1969), and supercedes those boundaries of ethnic origin, religion, status, rank or class, occupation, and age that fracture the adult world.

Each enactment of the *Alikali* masquerade is a *rite de passage*, incorporating the three phases of separation, margin *(limen)*, and aggregation characteristic of such transfigurations (Van Gennep 1960). The boys band together, building the *igberre* (devil house) in which their masquerader may be dressed in a privacy of their own creation, separate from the world of men and women. During the masquerades proper the boys collectively and simultaneously as individuals engage in what Turner has called rituals of "status reversal."

> ...when inferiors affect the rank and style of superiors, sometimes even to the extent of arraying themselves in a hierarchy mimicking the secular hierarchy of their so-called betters...the liminality of the permanently structural inferior contains as its key social elements a symbolic or make-believe elevation of the ritual subjects to positions of eminent authority. The stronger are made weaker; the weak act as though they were strong.... The [liminality] of the weak represents a fantasy of structural superiority (1969: 156-157).

The childish chimera dramatized by the maskers and their supporters is that of the fiction of the boy as man, the child as adult. For during the *Alikali* performances, the boys receive that most valued commodity of urban life—money—rather than giving, willingly or involuntarily, their labor as an assignee in an adult enterprise. They display to a wider audience and expect a public recognition of their *boldness*, rather than hiding behind their submissiveness to all those whose status, achieved or ascribed, normally requires a certain humility. Thus they sing of their own boyish skills and talents, powers and strength, rather than acknowledging their weaknesses and inferiority in that more rational and mundane world they share with grown-ups. They frighten and molest (at least in theory) women, dominate them instead of being disciplined by them—their fictive mothers. Indeed, in the world of the masquerade, boys and their supporters, in vicarious sovereignty, command men rather than offer obedience and fealty to their fathers who form an adult aristocracy.

The symbolic content of the performative and aesthetic patterns peculiar to the *Kaka* devil provides a further, even more graphic, illustration of the nature of these rituals of status reversal. For, in addition to its role as the antithesis of fine devilry, the *Kaka*—talking, rolling through the dirt in his worn costume, casually revealing the boy beneath it—is also a ritual clown. Crumrine characterizes this liminal figure as one "who utilizes imitation and burlesque to transform the everyday world into a sacred world of open creativity, in which normal behaviour is fragmented and recombined in fantastic ways" (1974: 869). As a ritual clown, the *Kaka* masker is obviously a human being acting as a devil—it is also a devil acting as a human being, but which particular human is it that the *Kaka* parodies so well? The following exegesis by a young Temne man clearly answers this question:

> The devil carries with it a cutlass as if he is going to fight or kill. A long rope is tied around the waist. The devil runs and jumps up and down in a wild frenzy, being restrained from causing havoc (of course the devil is harmless and does no harm). The name is a mockery of a lazy, effeminate man who only remembers and does nothing. He is a dog that barks and does not bite. The boy who is most variable and who dances or imitates a drunkard or crazy man is chosen as the devil.

The significance of the *Kaka* devil song, given below, is now apparent, for it has, as the theme song of the ritual clown, acquired a deeper meaning:

Devil: *Ah go fon don* ("I'll fall down")
Chorus: *Nor fon down* ("Don't fall down")
Devil: *Ah go Kaka* ("I'll defecate")
Chorus: *Nor Kaka* ("Don't defecate")

Dowdy and dirty, the shit devil prepares to fall.

Devil: *Ah go lay don* ("I'll lie down")
Chorus: Nor lay don ("Don't lie down")

The *Kaka* is a caricature of an adult man, exposing all the inevitable fallibilities that adulthood is prone to, for maturation is a process of decay. The *Kaka* ritual clown is the senile, incontinent, palsied apogee of adulthood, escaping momentarily, by defiantly but helplessly falling down against the wishes of the chorus, only to be led away in the end by its child captors.

If the *Kaka* is the clown, the Rainbow, *Talabi* and the Jolly are the heroes of childhood, and as such resemble:

> ... the fairy tale hero [who] has a body which can perform miraculous deeds. By identifying with him, any child can compensate in fantasy and through identification for all the inadequacies, real or imagined, of his own body. He can fantasize that he, too, like the hero, can climb into the sky, defeat giants, change his appearance, become the most powerful or most beautiful person... (Bettelheim 1977: 57).

Before leaving this period of marginality (symbolized but also induced by the masquerade) where the usual social order is upturned as devil-children impose their wills on human adults, the boys share a communal meal. As one informant, recalling the activities of his *Alikali* group, described it: "some part of the money is used to get foodstuff to be eaten together as a body. The preparation is usually done by the boys together in a place which is enclosed, made of palm thatches. This is to ensure and create a more friendly relation before and after the dance."

The social system which structures the relationships between members of the *Alikali* groups is, as outlined earlier, a meritocracy—that is, each official position is filled on the basis of individual ability, skill or talent. All boys within the residential unit are invited to participate, free from the strictures of achievement and ascription which dominate, define and ultimately divide the adult world. The masking group, as a democratic institution, not only enforces its own set of laws, but also formulates these very rules according to their own egalitarian ethos which seems to belong so solely to the world of the children. However, the children re-enter the structures of the adult, nonfestival field at the conclusion of a communal meal, when the devil costumes, carefully washed and folded, are put away; the musical instruments are stored for the season; and the *igberre*, which so physically defined the boundaries between the mundane and the masking realm, is left to disintegrate.

The masquerades are simultaneously a rite of separation, severing the connections between their creators and the social sphere of the adult, and a rite of aggregation, incorporating the creators in the culture of childhood. The performances, which comment both negatively on the world the boys are leaving and positively on that which they are entering, are indeed rituals of status reversal, but as such they emphasize and even dogmatize the very doctrine of primacy that they momentarily invert.

The devil masquerades are "deep play," and if fairy tales provide a literal text that may be read and analysed to appreciate more fully the psycho-drama they present, so too the *Alikali* performances provide a text or script for a sociodrama (Geertz 1972: 26-27). For they display, comment upon, and ensure the continuation of a certain relationship between the young creators and their parents, a relationship in which the boys are perpetually of lower status. The masquerades are art forms, generated by liminality, marginality, and structural inferiority, which provide their makers with an 'ethnic' identity as children, if Cohen's definition of an ethnic group as "a collectivity of people who share the same patterns of normative behavior, or culture, and who form a part of a larger population, interacting within the framework of a common social system like the state," is acceptable (1974: 92). The *Alikali* devils confirm that the boys are children, for men do not have these childish masquerades, but in the act of confirming their creators' status they also, of course, cause the boundaries between these two worlds to become more marked, for the *Alikali* devils are a *celebration of childhood*.[5]

Notes

The material for this paper was collected during in fieldwork Sierra Leone in 1976-77. I am grateful to the Anthropology Department and the Graduate School of the University of Washington for a travel grant and various fellowships and scholarships that supported this work and to the African Studies Programme at Fourah Bay College, University of

Sierra Leone, which granted me an institutional affiliation.

[1]Babcock defines symbolic inversion as "any act of expressive behavior which inverts, contradicts, abrogates, or in some fashion presents an alternative to commonly held cultural codes, values, and norms, be they linguistic, literary or artistic, religious, or social and political" (1978:14).

[2]Krio is a creole language widely used in the urban areas of Sierra Leone.

[3]Cohen suggests that charisma "is largely a group function, not an individual trait.... As a result, the leader is given, by the group, power which he exercises for the group. This power is normative in nature. It is essentially symbolic. The followers can with ease refuse to obey the leader without the fear of physical or economic sanctions" (1974:80).

[4]Girls are much less children and much more women since they are still rarely educated. This situation seemed to have also prevailed in Europe where "the particularization of children was limited for a long time to boys ... for boys were the first specialized children. They began going to school in large numbers as far back as the late sixteenth century and the early seventeenth century. The education of girls started in a small way ... and developed slowly and tardily. Without a proper educational system, the girls were confused with women..." (Aries 1962: 61, 58).

[5]As childhood, through the process of institutionalization, becomes less ambiguous, the *Alikali* devils may become children's amusement similar to contemporary North American Halloween, as part of what Max Weber called the disenchantment of the world.

Part V

Power Plays

Chapter 8

Barren Bulls and Charging Cows: Cowboy Celebrations in Copal and Calgary

Herman W. Konrad

The two communities examined in this study appear to have nothing in common other than the presence of cowboys as central figures during annual ten-day celebrations. One community, Copal, is a remote Mayan, tropical-forest village in southeastern Mexico, and holds its most important festival, of the Holy Cross, at the beginning of May. The other community, Calgary, is the rapidly growing urban petroleum capital of Canada, whose most important annual festival is the Calgary Stampede, held at the beginning of July. Following Cohen's (1974) thesis that public festivity is an important context of politico-symbolic interaction, I will attempt to show how the cowboy celebrations of Copal and Calgary represent cherished notions of identity and history which significantly affect the way that each community achieves, displays, and exercises political and economic power. I will also comment briefly on emerging changes in each community, and the way that these changes are seen in festivity.

The double-mixed metaphors in the title of my paper are intended to indicate two levels of meaning. "Bulls" are suggestive of power and potency, whereas "barren" suggests impotency; the idea is reinforced when we keep in mind that barrenness is normally associated with the female of the species, the cow. In the world of livestock breeding, a barren bull would not be kept, much less paraded in public, as they are during the Copal Holy Cross festival and the Calgary Stampede. The charging cows represent vested economic interests and power relationships in Copal and Calgary. "Cows" normally suggest peaceful productivity, resulting in good welfare (milk for growing babies, calves for aspiring 4-H members) and prosperity (larger herds), whereas "charging" is usually associated with bulls. Yet cows with calves frequently do charge, and when they do it is to protect their offspring and to promote their well-being. In addition—and this applies particularly to Calgary—a healthy market condition is considered "bullish" and competitors can be "cowed" through the manipulation of political relationships.

The overt public messages proclaimed by the Copal festival and the Calgary Stampede, like those of Disneyland and Disneyworld, cannot be taken at face value. The Disney enterprises are ostensibly for children but are actually for adults. They appear to be historical presentations but are much more of a commentary on contemporary American ideology that is legitimized by a manufactured version of the past. The same applies to the Copal and Calgary festivals: the former is ostensibly a peaceful, non-commercial, religious event; the latter a rambunctious re-enacement of wild frontier society. Both, in fact, are dramatic renditions of contemporary ideologies which legitimize manufactured versions of the past: in the case of Copal, involving an ethnic group's tenacious and frequently violent struggle for survival; in the case of Calgary, involving a past which was dominated by calculating businessmen and real-estate agents and in which cowboys played insignificant roles. Like the Disney enterprises, the Copal and Calgary festivals reflect the political economy of the societies that produce them.

Folk and Urban

Copal and Calgary, as population settlements, represent polar extremes in terms of scale, population, degrees of importance and integration within national economies, traditional versus modern lifestyles, and other economic, political, and social variables. Redfield's (1941, 1947) folk/urban dichotomy, despite the criticism it has evoked (e.g., Boskoff 1949; Foster 1953; Lewis 1951; Mintz 1953; Sjoberg

1952; Strickon 1965), provides a useful comparative and typological statement of differences between the two centers. Copal is rural, small, isolated, homogeneous, nonindustrial, personal—and the sacred obligations of community life are stressed in most collective activities. In this rustic village of less than 200 persons, all faces are generally familiar and related through bonds of kinship and common experience. Calgary, in contrast, is urban, large, intimately linked to the modern world, industrial (in terms of technology), heterogenous, impersonal, commercial, with the secular pursuits of individuals governing most collective activities. In this modern city of more than 600,000 persons, most faces encountered in the normal course of public life are those of strangers, without common links of background, experience, or kinship. The political economies of Copal and Calgary underscore their opposite natures.

Copal remains one of Mexico's most isolated indigenous communities, located in the vast tropical forests which at one time were inhabited by ancestors of the great Mayan civilizations. Recent pressures to incorporate this area into the national economy by facilitating (1) increased exploitation of its natural resources (forest products, agriculture, beaches, archeological sites— considered a natural resource), (2) the establishment of new popular centers, and (3) a more efficient political integration, resulted in a paved road passing within five miles of the village less than a decade ago.

These new communication links have completely re-oriented, without transforming, a localized subsistence strategy (slash-and-burn farming, hunting and seasonal chewing-gum tapping) to one of participation in wage labor, new consumer patterns and a greater loss of local autonomy. The frictions inherent in uninvited, forced integration of frontier zones, with distant national entities historically identified and fought against as enemy-alien, are still recognized by federal authorities and the people of Copal. Privately, adult males still express preference for political allegiances of bygone times when, via the English colony of British Honduras (now Belize), arms and encouragement had been provided by British interests, and when such military assistance had been utilized to defend an independent Mayan society. The symbol of the "great white mother" (Queen

Victoria) survives, although pragmatic considerations are
more pointed, in terms of soliciting good Winchesters (rifles)
for an inevitable, final confrontation. Publicly, however, it is
clearly understood that the Mexican future is here and now,
and that the real struggle is one of economic rather than
political alternatives.

In contrast to Copal's struggle to stay outside the national
political economy, Calgary, from its inception as a riverside
trading fort, has struggled in the opposite direction. The
railroad—that hard, iron, straight, politically and
economically inspired link between eastern, central, and
western Canada—allowed Calgary to grow and prosper. It
brought in the people who financed and worked much of the
livestock and cereal grain economy in its formative as well as
contemporary stages; it shipped out the goods to national and
foreign markets, and provided that vital east-west connection
which served to offset ongoing and potentially dominating
political and economic influences from the south.

Despite Edmonton's role as the seat of provincial
government, Calgary, has remained the center of the
province's dominant economic activities (livestock, then cereal
grains, now petroleum). With the emergence of energy
resources as a shaping influential national force Calgary has
not given way to competing centers of power (Edmonton or
Ottawa); moreover, Calgary's native son, Peter Lougheed,
occupies as premier, the 'dealer' role in the national 'high-
stakes energy game,' making major economic and political
decisions.[1] As a focal point of concentration of south-of-the-
border influence (petroleum and related personnel, corporate
headquarters, transportation and communication systems)
Calgary is both shaped by (e.g., the former "Husky," now
"Calgary", Tower, Petro Can headquarters) and shapes
regional, provincial, national and continental crosscurrents
and general directions. Federal Liberal politicians, waging a
national election campaign, come to Calgary not to win seats—
the complete sweep of the Progressive Conservatives is a
foregone conclusion—but to attempt to make statements on
national economic policy. The role of Calgary within Canada,
then, is in dramatic contrast to that of Copal in Mexico.

Bravery in the Bullring

The villagers of Copal, known as *los sublevados* (the

rebels) or *los bravos* (the fierce ones), retain a rich calendar of religious rituals encompassing pre-European Mayan and colonial Roman Catholic traditions (Bricker 1981; Bartolome and Barabas 1977; Villa Rojas 1945). During the annual festivities that begin on 1 May and end on 10 May, the most important during the year, *vaqueros* (cowboys) become central figures during daily afternoon bullfights. Each cowboy, a young man, is actually fulfilling a religious promise in honor of the sacred cross, the community's symbol of ethnic and ideological identity. There are also *vaqueras* (cowgirls) who participate in processions and dances. Such roles, viewed from within the participants' society, are sacred and entirely noncommercial. The bulls are made of a framework of vines, wood and sacking, with a carved wooden bullshead, and with a man within the frame playing the animal. The bullshead is of cedar, the wood of the *kuche*, which in Mayan means the "tree of the gods."[2]

The bullfights, along with religious services, processions, and evening dance, as well as special food for villagers and guests, are all sponsored by a deputy (*deputado*) and his associates (usually about a dozen adult males). The role of the deputy signifies considerable status and prestige and, in view of the costs involved, can be successfully filled only by individuals of wealth and importance. Since Copal is the sacred center of a number of dependent villages and smaller settlements (*ranchos*), it also has the largest number of deputies (half the total), all drawing upon kinsmen (consanguineal and fictive) from other centers. The sponsorship of the ritual events, and the costs and benefits involved, are similar to the religious cargo system among the Highland Maya of southern Mexico and Guatemala (Cancian 1965: Vogt 1969).

Cowboy performances during the celebrations derive from a combination of historical tradition and more contemporary models supplied by the fiestas of Yucatecan peasant villages. During the colonial period, when the ancestors of Copal were part of the integrated peasantry of the peninsula, Franciscan religious ceremonies and hacienda experiences incorporated cowboy activities into village fiestas. After the intensive phases of the nineteenth-century Maya military insurrections, known as the "war of the castes" (Canto Lopez 1976; Reed 1964;

Villa Rojas 1945), resulting in withdrawal of the survivors into the forests, earlier traditions were retained but altered to fit the new circumstances. Despite the resulting isolation, the proximity and occasional integration with Yucatecan peasant villages tended to reinforce the bullfight ceremonies, along with the greater emphasis on sacred Mayan elements consistent with the military theocracy and its sociopolitical structures. At present the historical legacy of active conflict and resistance against the outside have been reduced to more or less a posture of hostility and distrust toward outsiders (Bartolome and Barabas 1977).

The May festivities are still carried out as acts of reaffirmation of a holy, historic separateness. During the days of the celebrations, however, outsiders can be friends and even participants. These days, filled with social interaction, drinking, feasting, and dancing, are in sharp contrast to the harsh subsistence realities of everyday life throughout the year. This extraordinary period calls for setting aside normal schedules and activities. The festivities include everyone from the village, whose population triples and may quadruple for the festive events. The church, which is normally locked except for services, is open 24 hours a day during the period of celebration. The May ceremonies represent special conditions when the sacred and mundane domains of existence have no visible separation.

The all-encompassing nature of the bullfight is also expressed by the location of the bullring, adjacent to the church and within the bounds of the sacred center of the village, whose four corners are marked by wooden crosses embedded in stuccoed stone platforms. The participants move in procession, from the sponsoring deputy's house (after appropriate devotional acts), into the church for special prayers, and then into the bullring for the enactment of the 'fight,' then back into the church for more prayers, and finally in procession to the house of the next day's sponsor. Throughout the processions, prayers and fighting, music is provided by two drums and two violins, with the beginning and termination dramatized by fireworks. The physical location of the action thus reinforces both the ancient Mayan and colonial Franciscan structural arrangement of a sacred center within which important community events take place.

The fight itself requires a bull, bullfighters, and ropers—roles that are not fixed in terms of who occupies them at any given moment. The youth who starts out in the wooden frame—once inside, he takes on what he considers to be the bull's mental and physical characteristics—performs this most strenuous role only for a brief period (10 to 15 minutes), and is replaced by another youth while he becomes one of the bullfighters. Half a dozen or more participants become the bull, in turn; most take turns being bullfighters, and four youths, stationed on the four sides of the bullring (the four cardinal directions), lasso the animal at given signals and tie it to a center pole. Throughout the activities, which may go on for one-and-a-half to two hours, liberal ingestions of *aguardiente* (a low-grade, potent rum supplied by the *deputado*) encourage the bulls, bullfighters, ropers, and musicians. The structure of events and roles, like the structure of religious ritual, takes precedence over the individuality of the participants.

All males of Copal and its dependent centers will become cowboys at some time before marriage or during their teens. Some may fill these roles many times even as adults, publicly expressing the fulfillment of religious promises. All females, however, do not become cowgirls, and those who do so may fill the roles over a number of years. An older woman, who holds the title of chief cowgirl, instructs the younger girls and women. The cowgirl functions are supportive—marching in the parades and processions.

As symbolic action, the mock bullfights provide an opportunity for the males of Copal to express the historic bravery and fierceness of the rebel Maya, at the same time articulating the religious context of that struggle. In the past all males became soldiers who fulfilled their obligations of protecting the holy cross and defending the autonomy of these rebel Mayan tribes against outsiders. Today they are all expected to become brave bulls and equally brave bullfighters, thereby demonstrating publicly their commitment to community values. The larger battle against outside encroachment and the preservation of a lifestyle under stressful rapid transition is currently one over which the inhabitants of Copal have little control. Through their festivity, nevertheless, they express their commitment to the now idealized past. Thus the mock fights become both a

The Calgary Stampede: history on horseback

commentary on contemporary society and on an ideology which legitimizes a vision of the past

Cowboys and Capitalism

In Calgary the vision of the past is also subject to constant manipulation, albeit more closely linked to commercial and secular interests. Contemporary ideology insists that the cowboy represents the historical essence of Calgary. The city advertises itself as "Stampede City," and this image has gained credibility in the minds of young boys on northern Alberta farms, in Hutterite colonies, and in adult minds in such diverse centers as London, Quebec City, and Moscow.[3]

The city's Stampede, however, was inaugurated in 1912, over a decade after the demise of large-scale ranches in southern Alberta (1880s and 1890s). Despite its image, Calgary was never a cattletown in the same sense as were many American western population centers, which grew into major cities. The 'wild west' image suggested by the Stampede was the by-product of the creative imagination of a shrewd, hustling, south-of-the-border entrepreneur, Guy Weadick. It is not an accurate reflection of past local activities. The equally recognized Calgary "white hat," symbol of the city and now a part of the souvenir package of distinguished (such as heads of foreign states, royalty, even the current Pope) as well as undistinguished visitors, also turns out to be a recent addition to the cowtown mirage. The hat grew out of a promotional gimmick started by Don Mackay, a promoter, radio announcer and civic booster, while hustling the local professional football team (appropriately named the Calgary Stampeders) during Grey Cup activities in Toronto in 1948. During his terms as mayor of Calgary (1950-59), Mackay successfully institutionalized the white hat as a local symbol of identity. The popular view encouraged by the image-makers and advertisers, although loosely related to the city's historical past, is geared very much to ongoing commercial public-relations ventures.

Energetic self-advertisement and local boosterism have been part of the Calgary tradition since the 1880s. The advent of annual civic and commercial celebrations, today symbolized in the Calgary Stampede—the self-proclaimed 'Greatest

Outdoor Show on Earth"—dates back to 1886 with the beginning of agricultural exhibitions and fairs. The early fairs were accompanied by dog shows, baseball, circus acts, band music, horse races, rifle matches, athletic events (including a ladies' half-mile dash), and fireworks but no rodeo or cowboy events. The *Herald* (17 April, 1886) proudly proclaimed the local scene in terms of "the finest town, the finest country, and the finest territorial exhibits," while suggesting that "some energetic rustling" was needed to spread the message. The 1912 wild-west show put on by Weadick, with the financial backing of four wealthy businessmen, brought the cowboys into the act.

The early fairs established the tradition of annual celebrations, the first Stampede added the cowboys, and in 1923, the two were united to form the annual July event known as the Calgary Exhibition and Stampede. In recent years the agricultural aspects have received less attention and emphasis. Each year a specific theme emphasizes past (e.g., Century Calgary) or present (e.g., Salute to Aviation) events.

But the cowboy aspects always receive top promotional billing, as in one recent program boasting "world champion cowboys, saddle and bareback bronco riding, steer wrestling, calf roping, boys' wild-steer riding, wild-horse race, wild-cow milking and brahma-bull riding." The bucking and roping rodeo events during the Stampede, drawing upon amateur and professional cowboys from western Canada and the United States, form part of an annual rodeo circuit of similar competitions throughout western North America. The Stampede as a whole is designed to put Calgary on the national and international tourist map.

During the Stampede, cowboy imagery is expressed in a secular and commercial, albeit festive context, and normal activities (in dress, behavior and daily routine) give way to celebration. Business establishments emphasize western and cowboy themes in their decoration and advertisements. Individuals are encouraged to wear "western" clothing (hats, shoes, pants, shirts and insignia) and many do so. The local Hudson Bay stores, for example, allow sales clerks to dress in this manner only during the July celebrations. Western-style entertainment is emphasized in shopping centers, streets, and private residences throughout the city. Downtown events include parades, square-dancing, western open-air breakfasts, musical groups and drinking, dining, and dancing opportunities in bars and nightclubs. City employees receive a half-day holiday (on the morning of the parade), a practice also followed by some private employers. The high influx of visitors and tourists results in increased social interaction,[4] parties and a near collapse of productivity in downtown office buildings. The local media campaign to get everyone to visit the events at the Stampede grounds located close to the downtown area, where the main exhibition and stampede activities take place daily. The grounds are open from 7:30 a.m. until after midnight. The exhibitions are featured in the mornings; the midway, gambling, and grandstand shows at night. The competitive rodeo events take place in the afternoons, except for the addition of one morning performance on the last day. Only the chuckwagon races, perhaps the local innovation in terms of types of activities, and a major attraction, take place in the evening as a prelude to the professional stage shows which play nightly. The daily finale consists of a spectacular fireworks display immediately following the grandstand show—a fitting tribute to the feverish activity of overworked cash registers throughout the city's tourist-related establishments.

The planning, organizing, and running of the annual celebrations are under the direction of a nonprofit[5] corporation, the Calgary Exhibition and Stampede. Known locally as the Stampede Board, the corporation includes a president, two vice-presidents, twenty directors, and a host of hierarchically ranked officials—association directors, associates, committee members, honorary directors, and shareholders. At the bottom of the ladder are the shareholders, representing token rather than real ownership status, since the five-dollar shares neither pay dividends nor appreciate in value. Twenty-five shares are the maximum allowed, enabling holders to vote and hold official positions. The Stampede Board's work carried out by some sixty committees, each chaired by a director and involving a considerable number of the city's business, civic and political leaders. Year-round business, particularly financial affairs, are handled by a hired paid professional staff, complemented by 600 permanent volunteers. During the actual celebrations the number of volunteers and short-term or part-time paid staff increases tenfold.

The corporation thus includes elected, hired, and volunteer members. The ostensible rewards for the elected officials and the volunteers are the welfare and fame of the community and the recognition of a job well done. But the pragmatic reward seems to reside more in being associated with a powerful and high-prestige organization which fills many of the roles associated with exclusive and powerful private clubs (such as the Ranchman's Club or the Petroleum Club. These clubs mold the city's economic destiny via their corporate and individual economic and political decisions.

Calgarian participation in cowboy-related events is largely voluntary, although the local media and civic and Stampede officials attempt to popularize the idea that it should be one's civic duty to attend. They foster the myth that more and more Calgarians are attending. Despite growing numbers, actual attendance—in terms of a percentage of the total community—is falling off. The highest rate of participation took place in 1908, when four times the community population attended exhibition events. As the city grew, progressively smaller percentages of the total population have been participating. In the immediate post-World War II era approximately 50 percent of the population attended events at the Stampede grounds; in 1974, based on a study carried out by the Stampede Board, only 33.1 percent of the grounds visitors were Calgarians and of these only one-third were wearing "western" garb symbolizing their identification with the cowboy image. A small minority of Calgarians, it should be noted, wear western clothes throughout the year.[6]. The Calgary context and its lack of social cohesion—the media being the primary tie that binds individuals or forms a collective consciousness—in sharp contrast to Copal's pervasive social pressures, allow for a high degree of voluntary opting-out of participatory events. The Stampede thus becomes a pretext for not going to work, or at least not keeping regular hours, and for engaging in private, domestic drinking and other forms of socialization. Still, one should not overlook the phenomenon of "drugstore cowboys." Frazer described them as follows:

...harmless...go to country fairs, drink lemonade, make believe they are wild; dress in garb of cowboys, spurs the size of small cart wheels, hat cut with scissors and covered with mud...they race about the grounds...knock down old women...make themselves the laughingstock...strangers might take them for genuine and go away with a bad impression of country and cowmen (1967:55).

And when Calgarians take on the role of "drugstore cowboys," whether they go to the Stampede grounds or stage Stampede breakfasts on the university campus, with the president and vice-presidents serving the hot cakes and sausages to the clerical staff and students (few faculty members partake), they reinforce and pay homage to a double fiction: the actual historical tradition of the city and the real role the same individuals occupy in everyday life.

Perhaps the hardest working individuals during the Stampede are a select group of young women, the Stampede Queen and her Princesses. Apart from the barrel-race participants, the one event that is exclusively for females, they are the only decorative component for which being able to ride a horse well is a prerequisite. They must also, during the Stampede, always be dressed as cowgirls and virtually from dawn to long past midnight rush between fairgrounds, shopping centers, downtown mall, and official parties in an arduous round of public appearances, interviews, and presentations. Their roles, requiring serious dedication and an always smiling countenance, exemplify the idea that a "woman's work is never done," at the same time reflecting the true nature of male-female relationships in a city of male executives served by female clerical staffs. But there is also another side to the queen and princess cowgirl exercise, that of apprenticeship and experience for subsequent entry into the beauty queen competitions at provincial, national, and international events. Such pageants, always vehicles of commercial advertising, become reflections of the city's commercial and tourist economy.

The structural forms of Copal's and Calgary's celebrations are equally ambiguous as portrayal of past societal experience. But in the implementation of the forms as structured events, they become rather incisive expressions of contemporary

Cowboy clowns offer slapstick relief at the Calgary Stampede

realities. The collective community in Copal becomes reinforced by the re-enactment of the events, whereas in Calgary, the individual, competitive drive for economic supremacy is given freer reign. In Copal, a sacred ceremony serves as a leveling mechanism, reinforced by the redistribution of accumulated scarce resources. In Calgary, a secular celebration aids hierarchical differentiation, reinforced by selective individual appropriation of plentiful available assets. Excessive drinking, eating, and condoned violation of normative behavior occur in both cases despite the differing 'sacred' and 'secular' contexts of expression. Celebration indicates both what is different and what is similar in Copal and Calgary.

Copal: Festivity and Political Change

The most important person in Copal is the *nohoch tata,* or Great Father, an elected spiritual leader whose principal function is to see that religious ceremonies are properly conducted. He unites the functions of the Catholic priest (daily Masses, rosaries, baptisms, marriages, special Masses) and of the Mayan priest (subsistence, domestic, community, and identity rituals) in an attempt to retain ancient ideals in religious matters and identity, but he has little direct say in economic matters. He identifies the origin of Copal with Cecelio Che, one of the leaders of the "war of the castes."

His sons, however, represent the progressive forces in the village and as such, the *nohoch tata* encourages his four sons to become involved in the new economic and political order. They are the leaders of a new commercial honey-producing co-op and hold important local political positions in government. The *nohoch tata's* eldest son held the position of *delegado* (chief municipal authority of the region) for a number of years. During the son's day of responsibility the ceremonies adhered most closely to the proper traditional patterns. He provided the greatest amount of food and qualitatively better food (more meat, more dessert), more *aguardiente* and cigarettes than any of the other deputies.

Don Crispiano, who had been the *delegado* earlier, and who is also a deputy, represents the conservative forces in Copal, although he is essentially a pragmatist. He identifies the origin of Copal with General Cituc, a grandfather to his wife. He too would like to dominate the new economic and political order but is not in a position to do so. With no adult sons, his own involvement in back-breaking labor is substantial. As may be expected he resents the influences of the sons of the *nohoch tata* and opposes the outside influences they support. His allies are his kinsmen, with whom he plots against the sons of the *nohoch tata,* whom he cannot oppose directly because of his important religious role.

The current *delegado,* apart from the strength of this office, has little village influence. (The eldest son of the *nohoch tata* considers him a good-for-nothing). Apart from being the *delegado,* he does not hold any important village positions. He appears to be the compromise candidate, tolerated by the progressives, and accepted as a potential ally by the conservatives. Because he holds outside civic power, he cannot be involved in religious matters in the village. This is one of the Mexican constitutional provisions which has penetrated even the remoteness of the tropical forests. Thus, in the struggle between competing village elements we find a deeper political and economic struggle. The current *delegado,* being a weak individual, plots with one group, but whether or not he will be a factor in changing balances of power, is open to question.[7]

Cowboy activities in Copal represent only one facet of the annual Holy Cross Festival. Nevertheless, their fulfillment within the context of the bullfight has deeper significance. They dramatize the violence and conflict which was an integral part of the community's past history. At the same time, the peaceful and cooperative setting within which they take place underlines the sacred and harmonious elements that serve to unite this ethnic group in the face of outside incursions and disrupting influences. As long as the young men are willing to participate in these cowboy roles they signal their acceptance of community values and expectations. The sponsorship roles of the *deputados* are symbolic vehicles for articulating economic and political competition between factions. The display of resources by a *deputado* and his supporting kinsmen, measured by the amounts of meat, liquor, cigarettes, and fireworks they can muster, represents economic power and influence in a community that is becoming integrated into the national sphere of influence but which still clings to the ideal of a separate identity and rejection of outside forces. At present, both the conservative and progressive factions engage in the same symbolic actions while struggling for dominance. When the ideological cohesion of the community breaks down, as it soon invariably will, because of regional and national pressures, one or both factions will probably choose new symbols to articulate their economic and political struggles.

Calgary: Festivity and Political Change

The most important individual in Calgary today is undoubtedly Premier Lougheed, who firmly controls the finances and political fortunes of the region, the province, and, some fear, the nation. Before entering politics he was part of the Calgary establishment associated with the Stampede, having worked his way through the ranks to the position of director. One of the committees he was in charge of before moving to Edmonton and the provincial legislature was that of "Outside Entertainment." His involvement with the local Stampede organization provided, among other things, contacts, experience, and opportunities, all of which established a base for later political successes. Recently, when introducing Lougheed, the president of the Stampede board of directors clearly indicated that he felt his organization had played a significant role in getting Lougheed into the premier's chair.

The Calgary Stampede is considered to be a most successful enterprise and in the ideology of North American society, close association with one success opens doors to other successes. The Stampede corporation operates an almost year-round racing program, with paramutual betting; it runs a 21,000-acre ranch near Hanna, Alberta, where it produces rodeo stock considered to be among the best in the rodeo business; it has its own professional entertainment group ("The Young Canadians"), its own band and at times a hockey team; and it controls a fair portion of spectator entertainment in the downtown area. In short, the Stampede has become a big business operation.

Civic boosterism related to the Stampede provides a hedge against potential competing activities. The Stampede board takes great pains to incorporate the local media. Free passes, a special bar-room on the grounds, special receptions for the press—with liberal provisions of alcohol but not always food—provide, it is hoped, favorable dispositions toward the board and the Stampede. Political linkages with top-level media bosses, who instruct reporters to be positive and support the local celebrations, help ensure such coverage. The Stampede has the recognized status of "sacred cow" for the media. Many reporters do not like it; they grumble, privately refer to it as the "stupede," but continue to file essentially uncritical copy. One knocks the Calgary Stampede at one's own risk. Its myths about the past, the wildness of the stock used, the city's "wild west" heritage, its fantastic international reputation, the intrinsic Calgaryness of the white hat symbol, the total acceptance and participation of community members—all these items are accepted, perpetuated, and treated with great dignity rather than analysed or critically evaluated. Careful screening of potential critical input is also evident in the manner in which the Stampede Board conducts evaluations of its performance. Some recent assessments, for example, were contracted with the same firm that holds the Stampede's publicity contract.

Struggles within the rodeo aspects of the Stampede occasionally surface. Recently, for example, there have been disputes between the Stampede Board and the professional cowboys' association. The issues have been money (the percentage of the income from spectators which should become part of the prize money) and policy (who would choose the competitors in the events). In 1979 the board contracted with nonprofessional, "weekend" cowboys, thus nullifying its past claim to being able to attract large numbers of cowboys of "world champion" class. Losing the professional cowboy backing, the board immediately launched an intensive advertising campaign for a new approach, featuring "team" rodeo, "head-on-head" competition, and "interprovincial" (Alberta, B.C., Saskatchewan) and "international" (Canada vs. USA) team competitions.

Such changes in format suggest a deeper significance than a simple dispute between management and cowboy participants. The city itself has undergone changes during the past decade, affecting economic and political structures.

Traditional stepping-stones to political positions via memberships and directorships on the Stampede Board are becoming less important. The petroleum industry has become the dominating force, bringing in a large influx of new residents, largely professional, who do not always identify with traditional symbols. Some people find the cowtown image out of step with the emerging reality of a wealthy western Canadian city. New money and influence have begun to compete on better-than-even terms with the Stampede Board in the business of providing public entertainment..

In its attempt to maintain a high profile and gain access to increasing revenues, the Stampede Board has moved steadily into gambling ventures (vastly increased horse-racing programs with on-track betting, casinos, and lottery events). The new rodeo format, in providing a novel approach and "teams" with which spectators can identify (and bet on) will attract, it is hoped, more of the recent population that is engaged in a highly speculative and risky energy industry.

Celebration and Power

To conclude briefly, I have attempted to examine the interaction between symbolic expression and power relationships by taking two distinct regions and festivities in which cowboys play visible roles. Although the historical significance of the cowboy in both cases seems to be incidental or even artificial, the cowboy symbol is nevertheless an important diagnostic metaphor. A closer examination of that metaphor yields much ethnographic detail about the respective communities that facilitates a more precise historical placement of celebratory activities. In addition, the comparative examination of the structual components of celebration lays bare the dynamic relationship between symbolism and power.

Notes

The data used in this study derive from fieldwork conducted in the city of Calgary (started in the summer of 1974), and in a Mayan village identified here as Copal (started in the summer of 1976). Two long-term investigations—"The Calgary Stampede: A Western Canadian Urban Ritual," and "The Impact of the Chicle Industry on the Maya of Quintana Roo, Mexico"—are being conducted by the author. Financial assistance from the Canada Council and from the University of Calgary is gratefully acknowledged. Frank E. Manning provided helpful comments and advice on an earlier version of this paper.

[1] As a source of important political figures Calgary claims precedence over Edmonton, having produced, aside from Lougheed, Bennett, who led the Progressive Conservative party to power in the 1930s and Aberhart, who founded the Social Credit party which dominated Alberta politics for 35 years and has had strong influences in other western provinces.

[2] During a 40-year period (between the 1920s and 1960s) Copal had periodic access to cattle, and actual bulls were used in the bullfights. The use and non-use of real bulls correlates rather closely with direct impact of outside commercial interests versus higher degrees of village economic autonomy.

[3] According to a veteran Calgary-based CBC radio and television announcer.

[4] Local maternity wards also report a substantial increase in activity during the month of April, nine months after the annual event.

[5] "Nonprofit" in the sense that the corporation, as a legal entity, is obligated to spend earned revenues only on improvements and additions to its physical facilities. Its formal description is as follows: "The Calgary Exhibition and Stampede is a non-profit Corporation which leases Stampede Park and plant from the City of Calgary for $1.00 per year for the purpose of conducting the annual Calgary Exhibition and Stampede and its related operations, particularly stressing sports, youth and agricultural activities" (89th Report, 1974).

[6] This was before the more recent (in the 1980s) western madness in clothing styles which swept through not only Calgary but also Montreal, Paris, Berlin, London, Madrid, and Mexico City—all centers without significant "Wild West" or cowboy traditions.

[7] Recent information from Copal reveals that he was replaced by one of the younger sons of the *nohoch tata*.

Chapter 9

Political Powwow:
The Rise and Fall
of an Urban Native Festival

Noel Dyck

In the last two decades powwow dancing and singing have become popular pastimes among Indians in many parts of Canada and the United States. Weekend powwow celebrations hosted during the summer by Indian communities from Northern Saskatchewan to New Mexico attract anywhere from several hundred to several thousand participants. Together, these secular celebrations comprise what is known as the "powwow circuit."

In Western Canada the major symbols of powwow are drawn from camping, communal eating, and cultural performances based on shared aesthetic and social traditions. The weekend begins on Friday afternoon with the arrival of cars, trucks, and buses at the powwow site. The first night is taken up mainly by camping preparations and informal sociability. On Saturday and Sunday there are distributions of food to each family, a variety of singing, dancing and other musical events, many of them competitive, and ceremonies in which leaders, elders, and visitors are recognized and given money or presents. Powwow is deemed successful if it generates a "good feeling," an ambience of communal harmony, cultural pride, and a general sense of having been refreshed and rewarded by a weekend of spirited sociability.

Anthropological analyses of powwow (Howard 1951, 1955:

Corrigan 1970; Powers 1970; Lurie 1971; Campisi 1975; Dyck 1979) have endeavored mainly to reports its ethnographic form and functions, both as a type of cultural activity and as a circuit for such events. This concern with establishing the structure and general properties of powwow has led to its being depicted variously as a means for achieving cultural integration (Corrigan), a mechanism for fostering ethnic boundary-maintenance (Campisi), and as a vehicle that permits Indians to win recognition as individuals while at the same time generating collective self-esteem (Dyck 1979). Although powwows have also been recognized as potentially significant political events, this aspect has not been systematically investigated.

Social anthropologists have long been interested in the interpenetration of political activities and cultural performances. Gluckman's (1940) classic investigation of a bridge-opening ceremony in Zululand produced both a useful methodological approach—situational analysis—and an early example of how relationships highlighted in symbolic activities could be linked to the political structure of a complex society. Mitchell's (1956) study of the emergence of the Kalela Dance among African mineworkers on the Rhodesian Copperbelt also employed situational analysis to demonstrate that the general history of a cultural form or activity may tell us very little about its social significance at any particular time, a point reaffirmed recently by Cohen (1974: 3).

This paper combines a situational analysis (cf. Van Velson 1967) with an actor-oriented approach to investigate an instance where powwow constituted a vital aspect of political activity. Generally, I set out to show that cultural activity such as powwow entails not only a symbolic form that can be strategically manipulated by actors, but also sets of particular events that, when traced over a period of time, provide valuable insights into participants' changing interests. Specifically the paper examines the involvement of leaders of a provincial Indian association in powwow at a critical stage in their political careers, focusing upon their use of powwow as a medium for making favorable assertions about themselves and their political activities. Attention is then shifted to the efforts of these urban-based politicians to establish their own powwow within the circuit of powwows held in Western

Canada. An examination of these leaders' political activities reveals why the hosting of a powwow was initially an attractive undertaking, but one that could not, in the long run, be reconciled with their changing interests.

Powwow and Advocacy

The founding of the Parklund[1] powwow and the rise of the Western Indian Association (WIA) were inextricably linked from the outset: both were the achievements of a small but tightly knit group of urban Indians. Most of them went to Parklund as children during the 1950s from Indian reserves around the province to attend the federal residential school located on the outskirts of town. After attending school from four to twelve years, students normally returned to their reserves.[2] But in the early 1960s three former classmates at the residential school found jobs in Parklund. Before long they and their wives welcomed a few other graduates of the residential school and several other Indian families settling in Parklund to their regular weekend house parties and to their emerging mutual support group. Eventually this group gained a formal existence as the Parklund Urban Indian Association (PUIA) in the midst of a concerted campaign to have the regional office of the Department of Indian Affairs and Northern Development extend free medical-care services to Indians living in urban centers.

Seeking support for their stand, a delegation from the PUIA attended the annual meeting of the existing provincial Indian association, the WIA. The energy and determination of these young Indian spokesmen so impressed this small gathering of mainly elderly reserve residents that they not only endorsed the PUIA's demands but also elected two of their representatives to the WIA executive. A year later, when the Trudeau government unveiled its infamous White Paper proposals to abolish federal Indian administration (cf. Weaver 1980), members of the PUIA headed up the WIA's drive to rally opposition to the White Paper. By the end of the White Paper controversy the Parklund group had established close working relations with band leaders across the province and transformed the WIA from a small voluntary association into a sophisticated organization that enjoyed unprecedented support from reserve committees. With the advent of federal funding of provincial Indian associations' research programs concerning communications, service and research, several other PUIA members took key administrative positions in the WIA, extending the Parklund group's discretely managed control over the organization.

The role developed by the WIA during this period of innovation was essentially that of an intermediary or advocate who facilitates communication and dealings between band councils and the federal government. In addition, WIA leaders unobtrusively exercised their influence with reserve leaders to articulate a set of political objective on behalf of the province's Indian people (Dyck 1978, 1983). In the late 1960s and early 1970s the major political concerns of the WIA leaders were (1) to consolidate their organization's position as the representative association of the province's Indians; (2) to gather support for their policies from Indians and, where possible, from the Canadian public; and (3) individually, to retain their posts and offices in the WIA. In practical terms, however, the success of all of the above aims depended upon the ability of WIA leaders to retain unified support from the reserves which had permitted them to achieve so much in such a short time.[3]

Since theirs are relatively highly paid posts, WIA officials soon became the objects of relentless scrutiny by Indians. Leaders of Indian associations across Canada are familiar with the disturbing charge that they are doing little more than creating "brown bureaucracies." An additional concern for the Parklund members of the WIA leadership is the accusation made sometimes by disgruntled Indian opponents that they are urban Indians who are losing—if they have not already lost—touch with the grass roots at the reserve level. The Indianness of the WIA activities and of incumbents to WIA posts are, in consequence, matters of prime concern to PUIA politicians.

Before looking into the process by which members of the PUIA joined the powwow circuit, it is worth establishing just how appropriate a means for resolving their political concerns participation in powwow proved to be.[4] This can be done by highlighting some of the specific features and outcomes of the Fourth Annual Parklund Powwow, an event that I have described in detail elsewhere (Dyck 1979). Hosting this celebration cost members of the PUIA several thousand dollars and many months of preparations, but it was judged to have been a successful undertaking;[5] it attracted more than 200 performers and over a thousand Indian participants, earning its organizers many compliments then and later.

As well as providing the PUIA with a large audience, their powwow afforded them a near perfect cultural medium or vehicle for asserting their Indianness. Powwow is exclusively and definitely "Indian" in nature (Corrigan 1970; Dyck 1979). By hosting their own powwow they endeavored to show their guests that they were Indians who respect powwow and knew how to perform it properly, in spite of the fact that they lived in an urban center. In addition to its expressive aspects and hospitable nature, powwow was ideally suited to their purposes for other reasons. Unlike sporting events, powwow is an essentially uncompetitive and happy activity, within which their assertions could be made without risk of creating controversy or oppositions between themselves and other Indians. Moreover, powwow operates to reduce the geographical, linguistic, educational, and socioeconomic distinctions that otherwise separate its Indian participants; instead, it emphasizes their likeness and cohesion in opposition to mainstream culture and society. Through powwow these Parklund leaders interacted with reserve residents on a regular basis as fellow followers of the powwow circuit, rather than as urban Indians who are better educated, wealthier, and far more powerful than any other Indians in the province.

Powwow allowed the Parklund-based leaders of the WIA to seek validation of their assertions and legitimation of their identities as 'real' Indians from a cultural constituency made up of people at the grass roots of reserve communities in western Canada. The people who follow the circuit are not the temporary political representatives of their bands; they are the recognized adherents of a cultural activity that defines and celebrates Indianness as a positive value. To be elected to executive office in the WIA represents one type of support and legitimation for WIA leaders. But to be accepted as integral members of the powwow circuit and the fellowship of the powwow is quite another matter, and one that has major

significance for the advocacy practised by these Parklund
Indians.

Powwow provides these men with access to a network of
social relationships that span the province and with an
opportunity to achieve personal prestige within this cultural
system. As members of the Parklund powwow committee they
have attained personal and collective status as Indians who
perform powwow in a proper fashion. Moreover, one of them
has received recognition in western Canada as a dancer and
two others have had some success as singers. The powwow
identities they have earned for themselves and the
relationships they have formed with members of the circuit are
resources that are used to good effect in their political
activities. As Indians who have been accused of behaving like
bureaucrats, they acquire their powwow reputations to retain
some degree of personal integrity in the eyes of reserve people.

Powwow also serves these leaders as a forum equipped
with a medium for propounding cultural themes that parallel
the political platform basic to their advocacy. Powwow posits a
pan-Indian identity that cuts across the regional and linguistic
differences of Indians. Its emphasis on cultural cohesion
between Indians complements the efforts of WIA leaders to
promote political unity among the province's Indians by
means of the WIA. Both powwow and WIA advocacy are
founded on the premise of the boundaries and oppositions that
exist between Indians and non-Indians. Powwow is unlike
anything in the culture of non-Indians in western Canada;
indeed participation in it by non-Indians is restricted to that of
customers who pay to see it performed. Moreover, although
flag-raising is a common ceremony at powwows, at Parklund
the announcer offered an explanation of their significance:
"these are the flags under which our forefathers signed treaty
with the representative of the Queen, and under which our
veterans have served their countries." Whereas the Canadian
government discarded the Union Jack as the national flag, the
Parklund Indians resurrected it as a symbol of the treaty rights
and special status of Indians within Canadian society. The
Union Jack was placed in the middle and highest of the three
flag poles at the powwow site.[6]

The "give-away" ceremony was not unique to the
Parklund powwow, but here it had an accent not encountered

Honoring the Union Jack, a ceremonial reminder of Indian treaty rights

elsewhere in western Canada. Persons who were given gifts by the powwow committee at Parklund were of three types.[7] The first, "visitors who have come a long distance to be with us," are always recipients at powwow give-aways. But the second type of recipient—Indians politicians "who have fought for treaty rights all their lives"—constitute a distinctive category for recognition. In singling out these elderly reserve leaders, the powwow committee not only demonstrated a traditional Indian respect for the old, but also underscored their own respect for treaty rights and special status, not to mention Indian leaders. The final category of recipients included people who have distinguished themselves as practitioners of various aspects of Indian culture: an old Cree canoe maker, a Saulteaux medicine woman,[8] and several other well-known dancers. The most interesting recipients, however, were an old couple who received an expensive and finely decorated canvas tipi. Although these two old people were attending their first powwow, their presence at Parklund was defined as "saving Indian culture." Reading from notes, the announcer expressed the committee's hope that the couple would take powwow back to their reserve—a Plains Cree band located on a relatively isolated reserve in the northern part of the province—so that members of their band would regain "the powwow tradition that they have lost, but never forgotten." With this gift the members of the committee posed as cultural emissaries who graciously sought to share this valued activity with other Indians.

The unreserved applause that ended the give-away ceremony provided an immediate and encouraging indication that the Parklund Indians had succeeded in their efforts. During the remainder of the summer, members of the powwow committee were identified by people who had visited their powwow—and by some who had not—as Indians who knew how to make powwow properly. The Parklund celebration was evaluated by many circuit followers as a powwow that they would certainly attend the following year. As it happened, the next year's celebration, curiously labelled the "Third Annual Parklund Powwow," was the last held in that city. To account for the discontinuation of this event which had so admirably served its hosts' interests, it is necessary to retrace the steps by which the Parklund group originally joined the powwow circuit. The particular interests served by their Fourth Annual Powwow had not always been uppermost in the minds of the PUIA members; nor were they to remain so for long.

The Politics of Powwow Building

Although large-scale summer powwows have been held in western Canada since the 1950s, the Parklund celebration did not begin until 1969. Nor did it take the form of a powwow until several years after its inception. Indeed, the first "powwow" that members of the PUIA helped to host was not even held in Parklund, and was not so much an Indian gathering as a "media event."

In the spring of 1967 a senior producer from the Canadian Broadcasting Corporation (CBC) contacted a faculty member of Metis ancestry, who was teaching at a prairie university about the possibility of organizing a "teach-in" on Indian and Metis problems. The producer offered live radio coverage of the proposed event on the full CBC radio network as well as video-taping for later presentation on the television network; standard speakers' fees and expenses would be paid those who took part in the two-day event. Although the producer recommended that it be set up in a dialogue between whites and native people, planning and direction of the event would be left to the discretion of an Indian and Metis organizing committee.

Excited by the prospect of an event that would receive national attention, the faculty member quickly assembled a small working committee and drew up a list of potential speakers from across Canada. To enhance the television coverage he insisted that the "jamboree" include a range of sport and entertainment activities to ensure the presence of a large gathering of Indians and Metis. He also incorporated into the weekend event a parade to a nearby historical site of obvious symbolic significance—a battlefield where Metis forces had routed a party of Mounted Police during the North-West Rebellion of 1885. An appeal for help was dispatched to Indian and Metis groups throughout the province. The most substantial response came from the Parklund Indian and Metis Friendship Centre[9] and, in particular, from several Indian members of the centre who the following year would proclaim the existence of the PUIA as a formal organization.

To facilitate arrangements, the jamboree was staged on the grounds of a federal Indian residential school in a small town located approximately half-way between Parklund and the university.

The jamboree was only a moderate success as a celebration, attracting fewer Indian and Metis people than the organizers had hoped would attend. Although the program of baseball and soccer games, chuck wagon and foot races ran reasonably well, the brief powwow dancing contests—staged with a handful of singers and dancers on a baseball diamond—left much to be desired. Yet, as a media event the jamboree was a triumph. The radio broadcast was deemed "good stuff" by the CBC production staff. The invited Indian speakers made controversial statements and challenged the views of several local whites taking part in the discussions in a manner that made for interesting television coverage and film footage.[10] And for the members of the emerging PUIA the event provided not only valuable experience in the hosting of large celebrations, but also a close-up view of the workings of the broadcast media and the confrontational political style practised by several of the out-of-province Indian participants.

The following year the PUIA was fully engaged with a medicare issue and the forging of links with the WIA, but in the summer of 1969 the lessons learned at the jamboree were put to direct use. The publication of the White Paper on Indian policy provoked a near instantaneous and unanimous rejection of these proposals from Indian spokesmen across the country. One of the first and most articulate of these statements was issued by a PUIA representative on local television and carried the following evening on the national news. Ten days later PUIA members played a key role in hosting the Friendship Centre's previously scheduled "Indian and Metis Days" celebration at the exhibition grounds in Parklund. According to its organizers, this first ever celebration was undertaken to show the people of Parklund that Indian and Metis people were capable of staging a large-scale event and to foster friendly relations between native and non-native members of the community.

The schedule of events for Indian and Metis Days was similar to that of the earlier jamboree, featuring baseball, soccer and softball tournaments, pony chariot, chuck wagon and foot races; fiddling and jigging contests; and brief demonstrations on powwow singing and dancing. The celebration also included an elaborate "Indian princess pageant" or beauty contest, a parade down the main street and speeches by the mayor and local member of Parliament. Despite the collection of admission charges and the substantial earnings of the concession booth operated by the Friendship Centre, the celebration lost almost a thousand dollars. This loss and a fair portion of what would otherwise have been profit was accounted for by the powwow performaces; PUIA members had insisted upon offering generous prizes to competition winners and rationing all Indian visitors who camped at the exhibition grounds. Still, the Friendship Centre's board of directors was generally satisfied with the level of participation in the event and agreed that it ought to be repeated the following year.

The Second Annual Parklund Indian and Metis Days celebration was formally co-sponsored by the Friendship Centre and the PUIA. The event was moved up from the first week in July to the second-last week in June, a weekend when no other powwows or reserve celebrations were scheduled to be held in the province. The sporting events, princess pageant, and general entertainment activities ran much as the year before and realized an even healthier financial return. Nevertheless, in the words of the committee chairman, "the powwow was all expenses." A canvas "big top" cover for the dancing area had been rented from a nearby reserve powwow club and erected on a grassed part of the exhibition grounds. Experienced members of this club were also enlisted to advise the PUIA hosts on the handling of performance sessions and to assist in judging competitions.

The members of the organizing committee were pleased with the increased participation in the weekend celebration, but there was some dissatisfaction with its financial outcome. The Friendship Centre was permitted to count proceeds from the celebration as locally generated program funds that were eligible for a matching grant from the provincial government. Yet, instead of clearing a profit and earning a further matching grant to subsidize the centre's operation, the event again lost money, although the powwow performance sessions were noticeably improved. On the other hand, PUIA members expressed their concern that "certain members of the committee," notably themselves, were being depended upon to organize virtually the entire program. They recommended that the powwow and sporting events be held on separate weekends in the future.

The renaming of the celebration was only one of several basic changes made the following year. The Third Annual Parklund Indian Friendship Days celebration was again co-sponsored by the Friendship Centre and the PUIA, but this time the urban Indians focused their efforts entirely on the powwow. The remaining members of the committee took charge of the princess pageant, a baseball tournament, and of a cash bingo, included to ensure that the celebration would be a financial success. Other activities from previous years were dropped from the program.

Preparations for the powwow had started several months earlier when local wholesale-grocery distributors and a meat-packing plant agreed to supply rations to the committee at a reduced rate. More important, a man recently hired by the Friendship Center to augment its counselling and referral services was temporarily assigned to assist in organizing the powwow. This new employee, who had been recruited at the request of PUIA members of the board, was one of the best-known singers in the province. His personal invitations brought several American performers to the Parklund celebration for the first time. Moreover, he hastily organized a singing group consisting of himself, his father, two of his brothers and two members of the PUIA. During the weekend this group was introduced by the hosts as the "Parklund Singers."[11]

The number of visitors entertained and the quality of the performance sessions were exceeded only by the size of the deficit incurred. The powwow lost almost $2,500, with the result that grave reservations were expressed by some board members about the wisdom of holding another celebration in the future. The PUIA was not, however, deterred by the losses that the Friendship Centre had borne. The following year (1972), it independently hosted its Fourth Annual Parklund Powwow without accompanying sporting events.

It was generally considered to be a "good" powwow, in large part because of the attention devoted to the many tasks that hosting a powwow entails. Powwows held in other urban centers have often been criticized for their cramped camp grounds and for their proximity to major traffic routes. The site at the Parklund Exhibition grounds was large, well grassed and far enough from the city to make it resemble a reserve setting in at least some respects. Moreover, although it would have been far more convenient to have rented a circus-style tent from the local Exhibition Board, the committee instead hauled in poles from a reserve north of Parklund and spent two days planting these poles, bracing them with cross supports and then covering the structure with a canvas fly rented from another band. The "big top" at Parklund was, therefore, a "traditional" one, just like those found at the oldest established powwows in the province. The committee also went to the trouble of recruiting a small corp of Indian "powwows police" to direct incoming drivers to the camp grounds and to patrol the grounds during the evenings to prevent drinking parties from getting out of control.

Hospitality at the powwow was an expensive and time-consuming business. The oft-stated goal of ensuring that "the visitors will come back again" explains why, for example, one committee member spent an entire afternoon talking with visitors from North Dakota instead of dancing. This objective also dictated that substantial rations be distributed to the campers, including small but symbolically significant portions of frozen elk meat. Unlike the other items in the hampers, this so-called "Indian" meat had not been purchased at local wholesale outlets, but had been obtained by one of the committee members on a hunting expedition the previous winter. Finally, unlike other powwows where campers come to a central distribution point to pick up their hampers, at Parklund the committee president and vice-president personally delivered the hampers to each tent, identifying themselves to every family camping at the powwow site.

But it was under the "big top" that the Parklund Indians demonstrated that they were not only generous hosts, but also Indians who know how powwows should be performed. The committee's two announcers were sufficiently experienced to know when to call for the sessions to begin and when to end them. The committee also staged the dancing competitions under the direction of one of its oldest members, an

Competitive dancers at a Saskatchewan powwow

acknowledged expert on powwows who had recently moved to the city. He approached visiting performers to assist him with the judging of competitions and saw to it that proper decorum was observed within the dancing area: that children did not run across the floor, that spectators did not crowd too far onto the area, and that people were not allowed to dance without a costume.

The large number of dancers and singing groups registered at the powwow was impressive for such a recently founded celebration. Even more impressive was the quality of the individual singers and dancers. Several noted American dancers and a hoop dancer from Alberta were especially appreciated by the audience. The winners of various competitions were all "good" winners who consistently danced well at larger powwows. In short, the committee was blessed with the attendance of some top-level performers, an outcome for which the committee had worked hard for the last few years. The success of the event amply demonstrated that the Parklund Indians had become recognized members of the powwow circuit.

Two facets of this particular celebration that have not been specified concern its financing and organization. Experienced PUIA members knew that hosting powwow was an expensive business, especially when rations, facilities, and prizes were provided as handsomely as had become the custom of Parklund. Without the involvement of the Friendship Centre there was no ready means for writing off any losses as incurred. Some relief could have been obtained from a thousand dollar cultural or "powwow" grant available from the Department of Indian Affairs and Northern Development,[12] yet to have applied for one of these grants would have placed the PUIA in direct competition for scarce resources with reserve powwow clubs. Instead, in the three months leading up to the powwow the PUIA held a series of fund-raising parties to which many new members of the powwow committee were invited; on each of these evenings contributions ranging from five to twenty dollars were collected from each person. An informed estimate placed the total amount raised at these parties at over $3,000.

As the powwow weekend drew nearer, the PUIA committee grew larger and far less exclusive in membership than its parent body.[13] Virtually every Indian in Parklund was invited to take part in committee meetings held at the residential school. By the weekend of the powwow an impressive working group had been assembled.

In the fall of 1972, the election of a minority federal government triggered a new undertaking that fully absorbed the attention of PUIA members the following winter and spring. Preparations for next year's powwow were further delayed by the WIA's acceptance of an invitation to organize Indian participation in upcoming events to celebrate the Royal Canadian Mounted Police Centennial.

The first event was held in Parklund in May; it began with two parades—one marshalled by the downtown merchants' association, the other by shopowners at a suburban mall—that eventually met at the courthouse. An estimated 3,000 townspeople assembled there to watch the arrival of horse-drawn wagons and buckboards carrying merchants and employees costumed in western and pioneer dress and ceremonially uniformed RCMP officers mounted on horseback. Indian chiefs were garbed in feathered headdresses and combinations of moccasins, beaded buckskin jackets, and pendants; a decorated tipi had been erected on the lawn.

After speeches by the mayor, the local members of the legislature and Parliament, a provincial cabinet minister, a senior RCMP officer, and the president of the WIA, the action shifted to the lawn. Seated in a semicircle in front of the tipi, platform guests and the district chiefs waited while an Indian elder prepared a decorated clay pipe and prayed before performing the pipe ceremony. The WIA communications director provided a detailed explanation of the nature and significance of this ceremony over the public address system. This, he told the audience, was a sacred ceremony that in the past had been outlawed by the churches and government. The passing and smoking of the pipe was, he said, a gesture of friendship from the Indian people and a token of their desire for peace and cooperation with non-Indians and agencies such as the RCMP in the next hundred years. In the spirit of the occasion the ceremonially uniformed RCMP superintendent knelt to accept the pipe from the Indian elder, as did the cabinet minister, a Mormon lay preacher whose beliefs normally prohibit the use of tobacco. In conclusion, the chiefs and a number of costumed performers and singers gave a demonstration of powwow dancing that delighted the spectators in the courthouse square.

The main event of the RCMP centennial occurred in July when Queen Elizabeth visited the provincial capital. As well as inspecting an RCMP honor guard, meeting local dignitaries and hearing a series of speeches, Her Majesty was entertained by the most skilled troupe of powwow singers and dancers in the province. The highlights of the proceedings came when the chief of the WIA presented the queen with a large buckskin scroll with Indian beadwork and designs. The words inscribed on the scroll summarized the chief's message to the queen, a message that departed abruptly from the style of official greeting that participants had been instructed to deliver by organizers of the event. The chief told the queen that her Canadian representatives had not faithfully honored the treaty commitments that his forefathers had made with her great-grandmother. At this point, the public address system mysteriously developed a malfunction,[14] and the remainder of the WIA leader's comments were heard only by the queen. Nevertheless, within a few hours television-viewers across Canada and in the United Kingdom saw a videotaped account of the incident and heard the substance of the Indian leader's remarks.

The PUIA staged its annual powwow between these two official events. Beset by difficulties from the outset, it was so hastily organized that the advertising posters sent out a mere few weeks in advance mistakenly identified it as the Third Annual Parklund Powwow. When a PUIA member finally got around to arranging use of the exhibition grounds, he was advised that the rental fee had been raised from $150 to $1,000. Arguing bitterly that this increase might force cancellation of the powwow, the PUIA managed to have the fee reduced to $500. A far more serious problem was posed by the PUIA's inability to reassemble the large working group that had assisted in hosting the previous year's celebration. A number of local Indians who had performed essential tasks before, such as manning the concession booth, declared themselves to be unable to help.[15]

Nor was praise forthcoming for the current powwow, although it drew as large an audience and even more out-of-province visitors. Too much of the committee's efforts had been devoted to organizing the RCMP parade and not enough to greeting individual Indian visitors to the powwow. In order to offset the costs of the powwow, PUIA members also had spent much of their time hawking raffle tickets.

The election of several leading PUIA members to offices in their respective band councils sealed the fate of the Parklund powwow. All five retained their WIA posts and continued to live in Parklund, but their now regular trips to and from their home reserves left them little time to spend on social activities in the city.

Some three weeks prior to the time when the Parklund powwow was usually staged, local merchants approached the Friendship Centre to discuss how they might take part in the annual powwow festivities. They proposed a larger celebration to be called "Parklund Buckskin Days" and a range of sporting and general entertainment activities in which the whole town could take part. The merchants were referred to a PUIA member, who told them that there would be no powwow that year because the Exhibition Board had raised the rental fee for its grounds far beyond what the powwow committee could afford. This did not discourage the merchants, however, and they staged a powwow that year.

The last trace of the Parklund powwow disappeared the following year when a nearby reserve scheduled its own celebration on what previously had been recognized as Parklund's weekend.

Cultural Celebrations and Political Performances

The key members of the old Parklund powwow committee continue to attend powwows across the province and throughout western Canada almost as regularly as they did in the past; a few of them have assisted in organizing powwows on their home reserves. Each summer, then, the skills and contacts obtained in the course of hosting the celebration in Parklund are exercised and renewed. On the powwow circuit they introduce themselves as Indians from one or another band whose work in the WIA happens to require them to live in Parklund.

The rise and fall of the Parklund powwow thus illustrates a case in which a set of actors strategically manipulate a cultural form to pursue political interests. This much we may have anticipated discovering, given the skeptical bent of analytical questions raised in an anthropologist's mind when confronted with an activity hosted by politicians. The eventual demise of the celebration in Parklund also serves to remind us that although the interests of politicians may change over time, even a flexible and extremely manipulable cultural celebration such as powwow has certain fundamental organizational requirements that must be met.

Finally, this study demonstrates that actors' interests may not only be facilitated, but also revealed through their participation in cultural celebrations. The initial appearance of Parklund Indian and Metis Days and its subsequent transformation into the Parklund powwow parallels and, I would argue, partly accounts for the development of a small group of urban Indians into the leadership cadre of a successful provincial Indian association. Moreover, the relatively established phase of existence that provincial Indian organizations entered into in the 1970s roughly coincided with the crowning achievement and then the termination of the Parklund celebration. After 1972 the future of Indian associations was no longer acutely in question; by then PUIA members had also become powerful incumbents to WIA posts.

Having secured the support of band leaders through the implementation of programs that made band councils increasingly dependent upon WIA services, the PUIA members were in a position to pursue issues such as treaty rights claims and Indian control of Indian education. In their estimation these were issues that could be furthered most effectively through the cultivation of closer working relations with senior federal authorities, balanced with a selective use of the mass media to appeal occasionally to the Canadian public for its support.

In conclusion, the path that took PUIA members from a CBC-sponsored jamboree on to the powwow circuit eventually reached a point where political activities and cultural performances not only interpenetrated one another, but sometimes even constituted one and the same event. Powwow reputations do not, however, extend as far as Ottawa, although federal officials do recognize that officers of provincial Indian associations who are also elected band chiefs are figures to be reckoned with. As the practical objectives and political relations of the PUIA members changed, they sought alternate symbols and strategies to reach their goals.

Notes

[1]Parklund is a fictitious name, as is the Western Indian Association. I deeply appreciate the hospitality and assistance extended to me by members of the Parklund Indian community during the course of fieldwork that I conducted in that city during the early 1970s.

[2]Those few students who completed their junior or senior matriculation were usually encouraged to seek further training as teachers or as social workers.

[3]Efforts were made by federal authorities during this period to undercut provincial Indian associations by dealing directly with band councils. Specifically, the minister of Indian Affairs proposed decentralizing to band councils funds earmarked for underwriting the operations of provincial associations. He argued that this procedure would allow reserve residents the freedom to decide whether or not they wished to fund provincial associations.

[4]Powwow was, of course, not the only means that they employed in their attempts to resolve these concerns. In fact, the entire structure of WIA advocacy during this period reflected their efforts to deal with this problem (see Dyck: 1983).

[5]The total cost of hosting this event was more than $5,500; the bulk was offset by proceeds of a concession both operated by the PUIA at the site and by funds that had been raised by the committee in the preceding months. Nevertheless, there was a deficit of more than $2,000 that in the end was shouldered by members of the committee.

[6]The other two flags were the Canadian Maple Leaf and the American Stars and Stripes.

[7]The gifts distributed at this ceremony had an estimated cash value of $1500.

[8]The fact that she was a medicine woman was not, however, mentioned.

[9]The Parklund Indian and Metis Friendship Centre was established by a local Metis activist and a few sympathetic townspeople during the early 1960s to assist Indian and Metis migrants to cope with problems encountered in adjusting to life in the city. The counselling and referral services offered by the centre were financed by a small grant from the provincial government and the proceeds of small-scale fund-raising events such as bake sales and a weekly bingo. By the late 1960s the board of directors was comprised of essentially three groups: 1) interested whites, including several ministers, social workers and employees of the Department of Indian Affairs, 2) Metis residents, and 3) members of the PUIA.

[10]A National Film Board documentary film of the event was entitled "Powwow at Duck Lake."

[11]More than a few of the guests, however, identified the group by its leader's name.

[12]This fund became a mainstay for powwows in western Canada during the early 1970s.

[13]Although the Indian population of Parklund had risen from 10 families in 1968 to over 500 people in 1972, the PUIA membership had not increased proportionally. This influx of Indians into Parklund resulted from government policies to expand educational and employment opportunities for Indians. In summer 1972, Parklund's Indian population included 34 employees of native organizations, the majority of these being WIA personnel, 43 federal civil servants, 32 provincial government employees, and 76 Indians working in the private sector. Almost two-thirds of those in the latter category had obtained their jobs as a result of government "affirmative action" programs.

[14]RCMP spokesmen stoutly denied that the chief's comments had been "censored" by the deliberate disconnection of his microphone.

[15]Privately, several of these people observed that they would not let themselves be used by PUIA "big shots" who socialized with them only when their help was needed.

Part VI

Postlude

Chapter 10

The Spirit of Celebration

Victor Turner

Frank Manning has dealt most effectively with the leitmotif of this volume and dexterously interwoven the data and designs of the contributors into a coherent pattern of exemplification. Little remains for me to do, therefore, but to add a *coda* and a thread or two.

I ask myself the question: why is it that anthropologists and humanists have only recently begun to study carnivals, festivals, folk dramas, experimental theatre, rituals of rebellion, rituals of reversal, saturnalia, circuses, grotesque exhibitions, and many other modes of antinomian outrageous play, bordering on the chaotic? Is it really, as many are suggesting, that "play frames" have been burdened in modern "secularizing" times, with the "reflexive" tasks earlier assigned to "ritual frames"? Do we really look to these modes of cultural performance to confront ourselves, wherever we may be geographically, with images of our identity as belonging to unique indefeasible peoples, nations, cultures, and societies?

I am aware that there is a radical as well as a conservative reading of ludic genres: they are potential movers and shakers of the status quo, not mere photographic negatives, nor "safety valves" for normatively suppressed impulses against authority, nor ways of comically imaging the anarchy and chaos that would result if the established economico-politico-religious order were successfully challenged. Indeed, there is a *poesis* in carnival, as well as inverted *mimesis*. But I am not satisfied that any current interpretation hits off more than a fragment of the meaning of these paradoxical popular-festive modes (which, of course, differ strikingly from one another, though possessed of a common ludic core).

But why, I repeat, have anthropologists, folklorists, historians, literary critics, popular culturists, and sociologists begun, of late, to flock to the field of ludic studies? Is it the influence of Bateson's mighty mind in making us aware of "metalanguages" and "metacommunicational signals"? But the "metacommentary," even the "reflexivity," aspects of these genres do not account for all, perhaps not even their distinctive features. What of the coincidence in them of such opposites as orgy and organization, script and improvisation, reflexivity and flow, natural language and metalanguage, aesthetics and vulgarity, discipine and abandonment, portrayal and parody, acrobatics and clodhopping, heterosexuality and homosexuality, costuming and nudity, masking and barefacedness, lies and plain-speaking? This list can be indefinitely augmented from the lexicon of every language, both etic and emic (themselves terms rapidly becoming carnivalized in the anthropological underground).

The true carnivals are true to ambiguity. Once they become clearly defined, once they move into the indicative cultural mood of binary oppositions, mediations, and the like, they cease to be true to themselves, to be true to the bared human condition they so signally express and enigmatically represent. The politicization of the festive spirit of ambiguity and its channelling toward goals approved of by power hierarchies, secular or sacred, destroys this fecund ambiguity and makes of carnivals its own sanctimonious ghost.

Paleontologists speak of the "pediomorphic," "neotenic" characteristics of the most highly evolved (hence "mature") species of living beings, *Homo sapiens sapiens.* Men and women are the least specialized of life forms, except in respect to that extravagant mass of jelly, the brain (huge in proportion to the total bodily mass) and the weird foot that keeps us upright (rigid as many of our moral laws). The most mature is also the most infantine. In our genes, our bones, our softest parts, our mere physicality, is vested our ambiguity, our tenderest, toughest growth potential. That central nervous system of ours, with its archaic innervations, its cerebellum, its spinal cord, its cervicothoracic ganglia, its neocortex, extending over left and right cerebral hemispheres, laminated over more ancient regions, how it regrows our species past in every infant, yet gives it scope to play that past against the finest nuances of personal experience! So much futurity possibly resides in its unused jellies! Culture is simply the language-transmitted (including nonverbal languages) sum of each persisting group's most definite and determinate shared experiences, and the growing global culture the area of most apt interfacing of them all.

But culture's general character can shift, albeit oh so slowly, through the eons. Since the formulators of the great religions and philosophies emitted their paradigmatic messages around two and a half millenia ago, which became ritualized in standardized performances increasingly solemn and 'indicativized' in character, knowledge has indeed—in terms of New Testament predictions of "the last days," the Eschaton—been increased. With this increase in information there has grown an awareness of the infiniteness of possibilities both within us and around us, of interior and exterior space. We have become aware of the subjunctive mood of life and hence of culture, its mood of may be, might be, could be, and as if, and of how open we are to futurity. The solemn past may now seem, in the light of this awareness, a fetter on the playful future. Science itself may have become the mother of creative ludicity—its very lucidity the source of wonder at the complexity it begins to detect. Physicists discover a multiplicity of subatomic basic particles, to which they ascribe such ludic labels as "charm," "love," and "quark."

Mikhail Bakhtin, in his marvellous book *Rabelais and his World* (1968), argues that the popular-festive culture (whose humor, vitality, and vocabulary Rabelais was mostly instrumental in bringing into literature as a regenerative power), "the chorus of laughing people," is charged with the creative ambiguity we have been discussing.

> For thousands of years, the people have used these festive comic images to express their criticism, their deep distrust of official truth, and their highest hopes and aspirations. Freedom was not so much an exterior right as it was the inner content of these images. It was the thousand-year-old language of fearlessness, a language with no reservations and omissions, about the world and

about power (1968:269).

The "religions of the Book" (Judaism, Christianity, Islam) have tended to be more than a mite suspicious of this "fearlessness," this lampooning liberty, as have most political regimes, for the language of fearlessness recognized no definitional frontiers (theologically speaking) and was no respecter of persons, however powerful or holy.

Perhaps we are only now, we anthropologists and investigators of the human condition, beginning to learn the ambiguous, ludic language of what Bakhtin calls "the people's second world," a language as much of nonverbal as of verbal signs and symbols, always pregnant with good sense, always rich in metaphors and other figurative expressions, often scatological to counterbalance the chilling refinement of spiritual and political repression, but always charged with *communitas,* the lively possibility of immediate human communion. For decades we have sought in preindustrial societies germinal traces of those economic, social, political, and moral structures that we have assumed to have represented the true nature of the "social." Yet it has been borne home to us, through the multiple experience of our practitioners, that not only preindustrial but also peasant and proletarian social groups—"consociations," joinings of all kinds—possess a ludic richness in their chosen celebrations (even when these have in the first place been imposed upon them as religious or civic festivals), from which the literate segment of mankind may learn much that may be "conducive to its salvation" (to borrow briefly the smooth talk of many theologies). Sour disciplinarians both of the left and right, both atheist and theist, both clerics and commissars, have hardly begun to understand the performative genius of human beings (*nota bene:* I do not use the loaded term "the people") when spontaneously engaged in celebratory action.

By the nature of our profession, we anthropologists have been compelled (despite our almost universal educated, middle-class background) to live for years in close contact with the kinds of people who come together periodically to celebrate rites of passage, seasonal festivals, honorings of popular or local heroes, rituals of affliction, sudden good fortune, the public recognition of new leaders, and much besides. It is gradually being brought home to us that we have been in error, in 'bracketing off' such celebrations as "mystification," "false consciousness," "lower stages of cultural evolution," "ideological confusion," and similar pejorative evaluations based on consciousness of our own cognitive superiority. We have been all too prissy in wiping this 'dirt' from our fingers. To understand this 'dirt' is to realize its fecundity for thought. Not by stripping it of its concreteness as the Gallostructuralists would have us do, but by respecting the experienced wisdom tincturing that concreteness, a wisdom we can all learn and profit from, in every human ear. It is no accident that humus, humor, and humanity trifoliate from the same stem. This volume should encourage us to explore their carnivalesque expressions in further participant fieldwork.

Bibliography

Abt, Vicki and James F. Smith
1983   "Playing the Game in Mainstream America: Race Track and Casino Gambling." In Frank E. Manning, ed. *The World of Play*. New York: Leisure Press, pp. 50-65.

Apter, David
1965   *The Politics of Modernization*. Chicago: University of Chicago Press.

Aries, Phillipe
1962   *Centuries of Childhood*. New York: Alfred A. Knopf.

Babcock, Barbara
1973   "The Carnivalization of the Novel and the High Spirituality of Dressing Up." Unpublished paper given at Burg Wartenstein Symposium No. 59, Gloggnitz, Austria.

Symbolic Inversion in Art and Society
1978   (ed.) *The Reversible World:* Ithaca and London: Cornell University Press.

Bakhtin, Mikhail
1968   *Rabelais and His World*. Cambridge, Mass: MIT Press.

Barthes, Roland
1972   *Mythologies*. Trans. Annette Lavers. London: Jonathan Cape.

Bartholome, Miguel and Alicia Barabas
1977   *La resistencia Maya: Relaciones Interetnicas en el oriente de la peninsula de Yucatan*. Mexico City: Instituto Nacional de Antropologia e Historia.

Basso, Keith and Henry Selby
1976   *Meaning in Anthropology*. Albuquerque: University of New Mexico Press.

Bateson, Gregory
1958   *Naven*. Stanford: Stanford University Press.

Bellah, Robert
1967   "Civil Religion in America." *Daedalus* 96 (1): 1-21.

1977   *The Uses of Enchantment: The Meaning and Importance of Fairy Tales*. New York: Vintage Books.

Bly, Carol
1981   *Notes from the Country*. New York: Harper and Row.

Boskoff, Alan
1949   "Structure, Function, and Folk Society." In *American Sociological Review* 14:749-58.

Bricker, Victoria Reifler
1981   *The Indian Christ, the Indian King: The Historical Substrata of Maya Myth and Ritual*. Austin: University of Texas Press.

Buechler, Hans C.
1980   *The Masked Media: Aymora Fiestas and Social Interaction in The Bolivan Highlands*. The Hague: Mouton.

Caillois, Roger
1979   *Man, Play and Games*. Trans. Meyer Barash. New York: Schocken Books.

Campisi, Jack
1975   "Powwow: A Study of Ethnic Boundary Maintenance." In *Man in the Northeast* 9: 33-46.

Cancian, Frank
1965   *Economics and Prestige in a Maya Community: The Religious Cargo System in Zinacantan*. Stanford: Stanford University Press.

Canto Lopez, Antonio
1976   *La Guerra de las Castas en Yucatan*. Merida, Mexico: University of Yucatan.

Cohen, Abner
1974   *Two-Dimensional Man: An Essay on the Anthropology of*

Power and Symbolism in Complex Society. Berkeley and Los Angeles: University of California Press.
1982   "A Polyethnic London Carnival as a Contested Cultural Performance." In *Racial and Ethnic Studies* 5(1): 23-41.

Corrigan, Samuel W.
1970   "The Plains Indian Powwow: Cultural Integration in Manitoba and Saskatchewan." *Anthropologica* 12: 253-77.

Coward, Rosalind and John Ellis
1977   *Language and Materialism: Developments in Semiology and the Theory of the Subject.* London: Routledge, Kegan Paul.

Cox, Harvey
1969   *The Feast of Fools: A Theological Essay on Festivity and Fantasy.* Cambridge, Mass.: Harvard University.

Craven, Gerald and Richard Mosely
1972   "Actors on the Canvas Stage: the Dramatic Conventions of Professional Wrestling." *Journal of Popular Culture,* 6(2): 327-36.

Crumrine, N. Ross
1974   "Anomalous Figures and Liminal Roles." *Anthropos* 69: 858-73.

Da Matta, Roberto
1977a "O Carnaval como um Rito de Passagem." *Ensaios de Antropologia Estructural.* Petropolis: Editors Vozes.
1977b "Constraint and License: a Preliminary Study of Two Brazilian National Rituals." In Sally F. Moore and Barbara Myerhoff, eds., *Secular Ritual.* Assen/Amsterdam: Van Gorcum, pp. 244-64.

in press   *Ritual, Frames and Reflexions.* Philadelphia: ISHI.

de Moraes, Eneida
1958   *Historia do Carnaval Carioca.* Rio de Janeiro: Civilizacao Brasileira.

Dorson, Richard
1972   *Folklore and Folklife: An Introduction.* Chicago: University of Chicago Press.

Dumazadier, Joffre
1962   *Le Loisir et La Ville.* Paris: Editions du Seuil.

Durkheim, Emile
1915   *The Elementary Forms of the Religious Life.* Trans. Joseph
        W. Swain. Allen and Unwin.

Duvignaud, Jean
1976   "Festivals: A Sociological Approach." *Cultures* 3:15-25.

Dyck, Noel
1978   "Strangers in our Midst: An Examination of Anthropolo-
        gical Thought about Brokerage." In Richard J. Preston, ed.
        Papers from the Fourth Annual CESCE Congress, 1977.
        Canadian Ethnology Service Paper No. 40. Ottawa: National
        Museums of Canada.
1979   "Powwow and the Expression of Community in Western
        Canada." *Ethnos* 44(I-II): 78-98.

1983   "Representation and Leadership of a Provincial Indian
        Association." In A. Tanner, ed. *The Politics of Indianness in
        Canadian Society.* St. John's: ISER.

Edmonson, Munro
1956   "Carnival in New Orleans." *Caribbean Quarterly* 4: 233-245.

Elias, Norbert
1978   *The Civilizing Process.* trans. Edmund Jephcott. New York:
        Urizen Books.

Fernandez, James
1973   "The Exposition and Imposition of Order: Artistic Expression
        in Fang Culture." In W. d'Azevedo, ed., *The Traditional
        Artist in African Societies.* Bloomington: Indiana University
        Press, pp. 194-220.

Foster, George
1953   "What is Folk Culture?" *American Anthropologist* 55(2):
        159-73.

Fox, Steven
1980   "Theoretical Implications for the Study of Interrelationship
        Between Ritual and Play." In Helen Schwartzmen, ed., *Play
        and Culture.* New York: Leisure Press.

Fraser, William
1967   *Calgary.* Toronto: Holt, Rinehart and Winston.

Gamble, David P.

1963   "The Temne Family in a Modern Town (Lunsar) in Sierra
        Leone." *Africa* 33: 209-25.

Geertz, Clifford
1960   *The Religion of Java.* Glencoe: Free Press.
1964   "Ideology as a Cultural System." In David Apter, ed., *Ideology
        and Discontent.* New York: Free Press.
1972   "Deep Play: Notes on the Balinese Cockfight." *Daedalus* 101
        (1): 1-38.

Gluckman, Max
1940   "The Analysis of a Social Situation in Modern Zululand."
        African Studies 14: 1-30. Reprinted (1958) as Rhodes-
        Livingstone Paper No. 28, Manchester: University of
        Manchester Press.
1963   *Order and Rebellion in Tribal Africa.* Glencoe: Free Press.

Goffman, Erving
1961   *Encounters: Two Studies in the Sociology of Interaction.*
        Indianapolis: Bobbs Merrill.

Goldwasser, Maria
1975   *O Palacio do Samba.* Rio de Janeiro: Zahar Editores.

Goodman, Mary Ellen
1970   *The Culture of Childhood: Child's Eye Views of Society and
        Culture.* New York: Teachers College Press.

Grimes, Ronald
1976   *Symbol and Conquest: Public Ritual and Drama in Santa
        Fe, New Mexico.* Ithaca and London: Cornell University Press.
1982   *Beginnings in Ritual Studies* Washington, D.C.: University
        Press of America.

Handelman, Don
1977   "Play and Ritual: Complementary Frames of Metacommuni-
        cation." In N.J. Chapman and H. Foot, eds., *It's a Funny Thing
        Humour.* London: Pergamon, pp. 185-92.

Hardman, Charlotte
1973   "Can there be an Ethnography of Children?" *Journal of the
        Anthropological Society of Oxford* 6(2): 85-99.

Herman, Robert
1976   *Gamblers and Gambling: Motives, Institutions and Controls.*
        Lexington, Mass.: Lexington Books.

Howard, James H.
1951   "Notes on the Dakota Grass Dance." *Southwestern Journal of Anthropology* 7: 82-85.
1955   "Pan-Indian Culture of Oklahoma." *The Scientific Monthly* 81: 215-20.

Huizinga, Johan
1955   *Homo Ludens: A Study of the Play Element in Culture.* Boston: Beacon Press.

Hunt, David
1970   *Parents and Children in History: The Psychology of Family Life in Early Modern France.* New York: Basic Books.

James, C.L.R.
1963   *Beyond a Boundary.* London: Hutchinson.

Kaplan, Irving
1976   *Area Handbook for Sierra Leone.* Washington, D.C. Government Printing Office.

Kennedy, Sister Jean de Chantal
1964   *Frith of Bermuda: Gentleman Privateer.* Hamilton, Bermuda: Bermuda Bookstores.

Kochman, Thomas
1970   "Toward an Ethnography of Black American Speech Behavior." In Norman Whitten, Jr. and John Szwed, eds. *Afro-American Anthropology: Contemporary Perspectives.* New York: Free Press.

Kottak, Conrad
1978   *Anthropology: The Exploration of Human Diversity.* New York: Random House (second edition).

Lavenda, Robert H.
1980   "The Festival of Progress: The Globalizing World-System and the Transformation of the Caracas Carnival. *Journal of Popular Culture* 14(3): 465-75.

Leach, Edmund
1961   *Rethinking Anthropology.* London: Athlone Press.

Levy, Marion
1965   *Modernization and the Structure of Societies: A Setting for International Affairs.* Princeton: Princeton University Press.

Levy-Bruhl, Lucien
1922   *La Mentalite Primitive.* Paris: Alcan.

Levi-Strauss, Claude
1966   *The Savage Mind.* Trans. George Weidenfeld and Nicolson. Chicago: University of Chicago Press.

Lewis, Oscar
1951   *Life in a Mexican Village: Tepotzlan Restudied.* Urbana: University of Illinois Press.

Little, Kenneth
1970   *West African Urbanization.* Cambridge: Cambridge University Press.

Lurie, N.O.
1971   "The Contemporary American Indian Scene." In N.O. Lurie and E. B. Leacock, eds. *North American Indians in Historical Perspective.* New York: Random House.

MacCannell, Dean
1976   *The Tourist: A New Theory of the Leisure Class.* New York: Schocken.

Manning, Frank E.
1973   *Black Clubs in Bermuda: Ethnography of a Play World.* Ithaca and London: Cornell University Press.
1978   "Carnival in Antigua: An Indigenous Festival in a Tourist Economy." *Anthropos* 73: 191-204.
1981a "Celebrating Cricket: The Symbolic Construction of Caribbean Politics." *American Ethnologist* 8: 616-32.
1981b "Campaign Rhetoric in Bermuda: The Politics of Race and Religion." In Robert Paine, ed., *Politically Speaking: Cross-Cultural Studies of Rhetoric.* Philadelphia: ISHI and St. John's Nfld.: ISER.

Marris, Peter
1974   *Loss and Change.* London: Routledge and Kegan Paul.

Martindale, Don and R. Galen Hanson
1969   *Small Town and the Nation.* Westport, CT: Greenwood Publishing Corp.

Mayer, P. and I. Mayer
1970   "Socialization by Peers: The Youth Organization of the Red

Xhosa." In *Socialization: The Approach from Social Anthropology,* P. Mayer, ed. London: Tavistock Publications.

Merleau-Ponty, Maurice
1964   *Signs.* Evanston: Northwestern University Press.

Metraux, G.S.
1976   "Of Feasts and Carnivals." *Cultures* 3: 1, 7-12.

Mintz, Sidney
1953   "The Folk-Urban Continuum and the Rural Proletarian Community." *American Journal of Sociology* 59(2): 136-43.

Mitchell, J.C.
1956   *The Kalela Dance: Aspects of Social Relationships among Urban Africans in Northern Rhodesia.* Rhodes-Livingston Paper No. 27. Manchester: Manchester University Press.

Moore, Sally and Barbara Myerhoff
1977   *Secular Ritual.* Assen/Amsterdam: Van Gorcum.

Mount Forest
1977   Mount Forest Confederate.

Newman, David (ed.)
1962   *Esquires Book of Gambling.* N.Y.: Harper and Row.

Norbeck, Edward
1974   *Religion in Human Life: Anthropological Views.* New York: Holt, Rinehart and Winston.

Orgel, Stephen
1975   *The Illusion of Power: Political Theatre in the English Renaissance.* Berkeley: University of California Press.

Ortner, Sherry
1973   "On Key Symbols." *American Anthropologist* 75: 1338-1346.

Ostor, Akos
1980   *The Play of the Gods: Locality, Ideology, Structure, and Time in the Festivals of a Bengali Town.* Chicago: University Press

Paine, Robert (ed.)
1971   *Patrons and Brokers in the East Arctic.* St. John's, Nfld:

ISER.
1981   *Politically Speaking: Cross-Cultural Studies of Rhetoric.*
       Phildelphia: ISHI and St. John's, Nfld: ISER

Parsons, Elsie
1925   "Bermuda Folklore." *Journal of American Folklore 38: 239-66.*

Peace Corps
       n.d. *Notes on the Mende.* Washington, D.C. (Mimeo)

Peacock, James
1969   "Society as Narrative." In R. Spencer, ed., *Forms of Symbolic
       Action.*, Seattle and London: University of Washington
       Press, pp. 167-77.
1978a *Muslim Puritans: Reformist Psychology in Southeast Asian
       Islam.* Berkeley and Los Angeles: University of California
       Press.
1978b "Symbolic Reversal and Social History: Transvestites and
       Clowns of Java." In Barbara Babcock, ed., *The Reversible
       World: Symbolic Inversion in Art and Society.* Ithaca and
       London: Cornell University Press.

Peckham, Morse
1965   *Man's Rage for Chaos: Biology, Behavior, and the Arts.*
       Philadelphia: Chilton Books.

Powers, William K.
1970   "Contemporary Oglala Music and Dance: Pan-Indianism
       versus Pan-Tetonism." In E. Nurge, ed. *The Modern Sioux:
       Social Systems and Reservation Culture.* Lincoln: University
       of Nebraska Press.

Redfield, Robert
1941   *The Folk Culture of Yucatan.* Chicago: University of Chicago
       Press.
1947   "The Folk Society." *American Journal of Sociology* 52(4): 293-
       308.

Reed, Nelson
1964   *The Caste War of Yucatan.* Stanford: Stanford University
       Press.

Ricoeur, Paul
1971   "What is a Text?" In David Rasmussen, ed., *Mythic Symbols,
       Language and Philosophic Anthropology.* The Hague: Nijhoff,
       pp. 135-50.

Schwartzman, Helen
1978   *Transformations: the Anthropology of Children's Play.* New York: Plenum Press.

Singer, Milton
1972   *When a Great Tradition Modernizes: An Anthropological Approach to Indian Civilization.* New York: Praeger.
1977   "On the Symbolic and Historic Structure of an American Identity." *Ethos* 5(4): 431-54.

Sjoberg, Gideon
1952   "Folk and Feudal Societies." *American Journal of Sociology* 53(3): 231-39.

Strickon, Arnold
1965   "Hacienda and Plantation in Yucatan: A Historical-Ecological Consideration of the Folk-Urban Continuum in Yucatan." *America Indigena* 25(1): 35-63.

Sutton-Smith, Brian
1972   *The Folkgames of Children.* Austin: University of Texas Press.

Swiderski, Richard
1973   "General and Particular in Anthropological Theory: A Study of an Italian-American Fisherman's Festival." Ph. D. Dissertation, Princeton University.

Taylor, Julie
1982   "The Politics of Aesthetic Debate: the Case of Brazilian Carnival." *Ethnology* 21: 301-11.

Turner, Victor
1957   *Schism and Continuity in an African Society.* Manchester: Manchester University Press.
1967   *The Forest of Symbols.* Ithaca and London: Cornell University Press.
1969   *The Ritual Process: Structure and Anti-Structure.* London: Routledge and Kegan Paul.
1974a   *Dramas, Fields, Metaphors: Symbolic Action in Human Society.* Ithaca and London: Cornell University Press.
1974b   "Liminal to Liminoid, in Play, Flow, and Ritual: An Essay in Comparative Symbology." In E. Norbeck, ed., *The Anthropological Study of Human Play.* Rice University Studies, 60: 53-92.
1977   "Variations on a Theme of Liminality." In S. F. Moore and B. Myerhoff, eds., *Secular Ritual.* Assen/Amsterdam: Van

Gorcum, pp. 36-52.
1978a   Foreword in Barbara Myerhoff, *Number Our Days*. New York:
Simon and Shuster, pp. xiii-xvii.
1978b   *Image and Pilgrimage in Christian Culture*. New York:
Columbia University.

Van Gennep, Arnold
1960   *The Rites of Passage*. Trans. Monika Vizedom and Gabrielle
L. Coffee. London: Routledge and Kegan Paul.

Van Velson, J.
1967   "The Extended-case Method and Situational Analysis." In
A. L. Epstein, ed., *The Craft of Social Anthropology*. London:
Tavistock Publications, pp. 129-49.

Villa Rojas, Alfonso
1945   *The Maya of East Central Quintana Roo*. Washington: Carne-
gie Institution of Washington, Publication #559.

Vogt, Evon
1969   *Zinacantan: A Maya Community in the Highlands of Chiapas*.
Cambridge, Mass.: Harvard University Press.

Warner, W. Lloyd
1953   *American Life: Dream and Reality*. Chicago: Univ. of Chicago
Press.
1959   *The Living and the Dead: A Study of the Symbolic Life of
the Americans*. Volume V: Yankee City Series.
New Haven: Yale University Press.

Weaver, Sally M.
1980   *The Hidden Agenda: Indian Policy and the Trudeau Government*. Toronto: University of Toronto Press.

Weber, Max
1958   *The Protestant Ethic and the Spirit of Capitalism*. Trans.
Talcott Parsons. New York: Scribners.

Welch, Charles
1970   *Oh Dem Golden Slippers*. New York: Thomas Nelson.

Wilson, Peter
1973   *Crab Antics: The Social Anthropology of English Speaking
Negro Societies of the Caribbean*. New Haven and London:
Yale University Press.

Wolfe, Tom
1966   *The Kandy-Kolored Tangerine Flake Streamline Baby.* New York: Pocket Books.

Wright, A.
1927   "Memories of Mount Forest and the Surrounding Townships, Minto, Arthur, West Luther, Normanby, Egremont and Proton, in honour of the Diamond Jubilee of the Confederation and Dominion of Canada, etc." Mount Forest: Mount Forest Confederate.

Author Index

Subject Index

187-92
theories of, 14, 85-90, 104-12
politics:
  as aspect of social organization, 38, 42-48
    159-63
  as component of celebration, 3-4, 7, 12-20,
    27-30, 34-35, 42-49, 75, 79, 81, 90, 94-99,
    115, 117, 131, 135-40, 145-84
Protestantism, influence of, 13, 21, 23-25,
  38, 53, 81, 97-98

radio, *see* broadcast media
Rio de Janeiro, 3, 14-15, 21-22, 26, 28, 51,
  103-24
rites of passage, 8, 10, 41, 136, 140, 190
ritual:
  As symbolic frame, 7, 20-30, 105, 187-92

rituals of reversal, *see* inversion

samba schools, 14-15, 110-22
Saskatchewan, 19, 165-84
sex:
  sex roles, 10, 20, 21, 54-57, 61-64, 123,
    127-29, 133, 151, 157
  sexual license, 12, 15, 21, 47, 87-90, 111,
    114, 121-22, 159, 164n, 188
Simcoe, Ontario, 67-79
situational analysis, 166

television, *see* broadcast media
'text', as analytical model, 6-7, 14, 35, 51-52,
  56, 61-64, 98, 140
tourist attractions, 10, 18, 26, 40, 58-64, 104,
  154, 157, 165